What Works in Distance Learning

Guidelines

What Works in Distance Learning
Guidelines

Edited by

Harold F. O'Neil
University of Southern California/CRESST

INFORMATION AGE
PUBLISHING

80 Mason Street • Greenwich, Connecticut 06830 • www.infoagepub.com

Library of Congress Cataloging-in-Publication Data

What works in distance learning : guidelines / edited by Harold F.
O'Neil.
    p. cm.
    Includes bibliographical references.
    ISBN 1-59311-260-2 (pbk.) – ISBN 1-59311-261-0 (hardcover)
    1. Distance education. I. O'Neil, Harold F., 1943-
    LC5800.W54 2005
    371.35–dc22

                                                                2004025837

Printed in the United States of America

CONTENTS

CHAPTER 1

BACKGROUND AND PURPOSE[1]

Harold F. O'Neil
University of Southern California/CRESST

Eva L. Baker and William Bewley
UCLA/CRESST

The purpose of this book is to document our progress to date in what works in distance learning (DL). An overriding goal of this effort was to create a robust and clear set of design guidelines to support the next generation of DL training.

The basic methodology in developing the guidelines consisted of a research synthesis conducted by experts, using analytical methods, on what is known about what works in distance learning. Research in the literature was reviewed for design flaws, and only studies with robust designs were included. Also, we included only those entries for which research evidence and expert opinion were stable and consistent. Furthermore, we decided that this information would be provided to researchers, instructors, program managers, and instructional or assessment designers in a "What Works" format, that is, *What Works in Distance Learning*. We adopted many of the conventions of *What Works: Research About Teaching and Learning* (U.S. Department of Education, 1986, 1987).

There are several types of documentation provided for our overall *What Works* effort. The first is this book, which documents the rationale and

What Works in Distance Learning: Guidlines, pages 1–6
Copyright © 2005 by Information Age Publishing
All rights of reproduction in any form reserved.

approach, provides the guidelines, and addresses implementation issues. The book is targeted mainly toward the research and program management communities. A companion book contains a set of lessons that are organized by guideline area. These lessons depict specific guideline areas in terms of how a particular guideline would look instantiated in a lesson. The lessons are formatted as a case (Mayer, 2003) or partially worked example (Kalyuga, Chandler, Touvinen, & Sweller, 2001).

With respect to guidelines per se, a considerable challenge exists in integrating knowledge from diverse sources into a set of comprehensive, coherent, and useful distance learning guidelines and applying those guidelines to the development and application of distance learning components. There are five critical dimensions of the distance learning system we support with guideline references: multimedia strategies, learner characteristics (including learning strategies, motivational strategies, and self-regulation strategies), instructional strategies, assessment strategies, and management strategies.

These strategies were chosen based on our analysis of competing instructional models historically used in training and education. By analyzing the strengths and weaknesses of each model, we were able to indicate which of its attributes should be moved forward as candidate elements for a new set of design principles to support distance learning. Following this analysis, we provided a top-level view of the attributes of an instructional model. Among the archetypal models containing elements from which the new instructional model could be constructed, we selected the following: gifted teacher/mentor/tutor, instructional systems development, computer-assisted instruction/embedded systems, and intelligent tutoring systems.

The gifted teacher/mentor/tutor model (Bloom, 1984; Shuell, 1996) has the longest and most revered tradition in teaching and learning, and at its best, involves teacher/mentors that possess deep content understanding, high pedagogical knowledge, insight into the needs of particular students, and the ability to encourage and motivate. What these mentors do is personal and unique, however; it cannot be easily replicated or scaled up.

The instructional systems development model (O'Neil, 1997a, 1997b; Reigeluth, 1999), on the other hand, provides guidelines for systematizing and scaling up instructional delivery. At its best, the instructional systems development model produces rules that are empirically derived and uses the extant research base in psychology and learning as a source of recommendations on methods such as advance organizers, practice, feedback, and sequencing. Instructional systems development's limitation, however, is that it has tended to become overly routinized, orthodox, and rigid, leading to rules that are arbitrary and inadequately reflective of contemporary research.

The computer-assisted instruction/simulation systems model (O'Neil & Andrews, 2000) represents an attempt to apply some aspects of the instructional systems development model in advanced technology settings, including full- and part-task simulations. Much of computer-assisted instruction, however, has not taken advantage of recent research on learning and assessment, and computer-assisted instruction often exemplifies a routinized "ask-present-ask-present-ask" sequence that is unlikely to sustain high interest over time.

Finally, intelligent tutoring systems components (Fletcher, 2003; Regian & Shute, 1994) have been used in various contexts, ranging from adaptive individual tutors to natural language systems for understanding student responses or messages. Intelligent tutoring systems approaches have raised the salience of detailed analyses of content and skills to be learned, focused on the ideal attributes of adaptive instruction, and highlighted the role that compiled expertise can play in the design and operation of a variety of systems. At present, the limitation of intelligent tutoring systems relates to scalability. Domains of interest in intelligent tutoring systems tend to be very narrow, and large-scale development of intelligent tutoring systems is inhibited by cost, technology demands, and expertise.

Nevertheless, our analysis of instructional efforts illustrates that each of the four archetypes has elements or features that are desirable and can begin to define the design space for distance learning guidelines. From the gifted teacher/mentor/tutor archetype, we identify the importance of motivational and social supports designed to assist learners and sustain their commitment to education. From instructional systems development we identify the importance of deriving clear instructional strategies and assessments and attending to the notion of flexible scalability of future systems. From the computer-assisted instruction/simulation systems model, we extrapolate the importance of learning in context and the role of learning strategies for adult learners. From intelligent tutoring systems models we bring the importance of adaptation based on student needs, the importance of domain specification, and the importance of mapping cognitive demands appropriately to task design. From extant research on these models, then, we extracted one or more useful guidelines for specifying the critical dimensions of the distance learning.

SPECIFIC METHODOLOGY

Our guidelines production strategy involved the following steps: (1) use experts to compile knowledge; (2) use a standardized format for the guidelines, which requires a scientific base; (3) create a paper version; and (4) transition to the training and education community. Our goal for nonresearchers was to translate the research findings into clear and comprehensible statements or guidelines that we think can help users to guide their practice. The following format conventions for guidelines are quoted from Montague (1988). The report will "be organized into sections presenting the research synopses. Each gives a short statement presenting the research findings of practical value for the user group. A comment section explains more about the findings and how one might implement conditions that should lead to similar results. References are included for readers who might be interested in the evidence supporting the finding or, in some cases, describing detailed procedures for implementation" (p. 2). These format constraints are the same as those used in *What Works: Research About Teaching and Learning* (U.S. Department of Education, 1986, 1987). Our modifications for the guidelines format consisted of adding (1) a brief section specifying whether a guideline was based on research or expert opinion, (2) a brief rating of the degree of our confidence in the guideline (high, medium, or low), (3) a glossary of terms used, and (4) an indication of the role(s) of the primary users to whom the guideline is addressed. An earlier version of these guidelines can be found in a technical report (O'Neil, 2003) and at www.adlnet.org/index.cfm?fuseaction=DLGuid, the website of the Advanced Distributed Learning Initiative, sponsored by the Office of the Secretary of Defense, U.S. Department of Defense.

Our guidelines specifications that the experts used to generate the distance learning guidelines are shown in Figure 1.1.

We developed the following core group of research-based distance learning guidelines for seven key areas: (1) Multimedia Strategies, by Richard Mayer; (2) Instructional Strategies, by Richard Clark; (3) Learning Strategies, by Myron Dembo and Linda Gubler Junge; (4) Assessment Strategies, by Eva Baker, Zenaida Aguirre-Muñoz, Jia Wang, and David Niemi; (5) Motivation Strategies, by Richard Clark; (6) Self-Regulation Strategies by Harold O'Neil and Sanhui (Sabrina) Chuang; and (7) Management Strategies, by Edward Kazlauskas. Each set of guidelines was edited by Harry O'Neil and revised by the author(s). Next, each set was copy edited and then reviewed and approved by the author(s). The order of the guidelines within each set is arbitrary.

The remaining chapters in this book provide the guidelines for each of the seven key areas and a discussion of transition and implementation issues.

Title of Guideline[1,2]

Section	Definition/Function
1. Guideline:	One- or two-sentence overview of findings. What would you tell a smart but not technically oriented significant other about the area.
2. Guideline based on:	Research or expert opinion.
3. Degree of confidence:	Your degree of confidence in the guideline. Low, medium, high (if no empirical evidence, the high-confidence category cannot be used).
4. Comments:	Two to three paragraphs about the findings. Could include more detail and ways to implement the guideline to lead to similar findings. Best evidence would be empirical.
5. References:	Three to four APA-style references. These are provided for users who want more detail. One of the references should be seminal (defined area or key terms, scholar that represents area, etc.). One reference should be to a literature review in the area. A meta-analysis would provide the best evidence. The remaining references should be to recent journal articles or to sources someone could easily find (e.g., no conference presentations, dissertations, technical reports, etc.). Minimal reference to books, because of expense of buying books.
6. Glossary:	One-sentence definitions (with reference) of all jargon on the page.
7. User:	For whom did you write the guideline (e.g., instructional designer or program manager)?

[1] Design Specifications: DL Guidelines (maximum 2 pages, single-spaced).
[2] Include version number, date, and page numbers in document header.

Figure 1.1.

NOTE

1. The work reported in this book was supported under Office of Naval Research Award No. N00014-02-1-0179 to the National Center for Research on Evaluation, Standards, and Student Testing (CRESST), as administered by the Office of Naval Research, and under the Educational Research and Development Centers Program, PR/Award No. R305B960002, as administered by the Institute of Education Sciences (IES), U.S. Department of Education. The findings and opinions expressed in this publication do not reflect the positions or policies of the Office of Naval Research, the National Center for Education Research, the Institute of Education Sciences, or the U.S. Department of Education.

REFERENCES

Bloom, B. S. (1984). The 2 Sigma problem: The search for methods of group instruction as effective as one-to-one tutoring. *Educational Researcher, 13*(6), 4–15.

Fletcher, J. D. (2003) Evidence for learning from technology-assisted instruction. In H. F. O'Neil Jr., & R. Perez (Eds.) *Technology applications in education: A learning view* (pp. 79–99). Mahwah, NJ: Erlbaum.

Kalyuga, S., Chandler, P., Touvinen, J., & Sweller, J. (2001). When problem solving is superior to worked examples. *Journal of Educational Psychology, 93*, 579–588.

Mayer, R. E. (2003). *Learning and instruction.* Upper Saddle River, NJ: Pearson Education.

Montague, W. E. (Ed.). (1988). *What works: Summary of research findings with implications for Navy instruction and learning.* Pensacola, FL: Office of the Chief of Naval Education and Training.

O'Neil, H. F., Jr. (Ed.). (1979a). *Issues in instructional systems development.* New York: Academic Press.

O'Neil, H. F., Jr. (Ed.). (1979b). *Procedures for instructional systems development.* New York: Academic Press.

O'Neil, H. F. (Ed.). (2003). *What works in distance learning* (Report to the Office of Naval Research). Los Angeles: University of Southern California, Rossier School of Education. Available at www.adlnet.org/index.cfm?fuseaction =DLGuid

O'Neil, H. F., Jr., & Andrews, D. (Eds.). (2000). *Aircrew training and assessment.* Mahwah, NJ: Erlbaum.

Regian, J. W., & Shute, V. J. (1994). Evaluating intelligent tutoring systems. In E. L. Baker & H. F. O'Neil, Jr. (Eds.), *Technology assessment in education and training* (pp. 79–96). Hillsdale, NJ: Erlbaum.

Reigeluth, C. M. (Ed.). (1999). *Instructional-design theories and models: Vol II.* Mahwah, NJ: Erlbaum.

Shuell, T. J. (1996). Teaching and learning in a classroom context. In D. C. Berliner & R. C. Calfee (Eds.), *Handbook of educational psychology* (pp. 726–764). New York: Simon & Schuster Macmillan.

U.S. Department of Education. (1986). *What works: Research about teaching and learning.* Washington, DC: U.S. Government Printing Office.

U.S. Department of Education. (1987). *What works: Research about teaching and learning* (2nd ed., IS 87-110). Washington, DC: U.S. Government Printing Office.

CHAPTER 2

MULTIMEDIA STRATEGIES

Richard E. Mayer
University of California, Santa Barbara

The following guidelines are presented in this chapter:

Strategies Based on the Coherence Principle
Strategies Based on the Modality Principle
Strategies Based on the Multimedia Principle
Strategies Based on the Personalization Principle
Strategies Based on the Pre-Training Principle
Strategies Based on the Prior Knowledge Principle
Strategies Based on the Redundancy Principle
Strategies Based on the Signaling Principle
Strategies Based on the Spatial Contiguity Principle
Strategies Based on the Temporal Contiguity Principle
Strategies Based on the Voice Principle

What Works in Distance Learning: Guidlines, pages 7–23
Copyright © 2005 by Information Age Publishing

STRATEGIES BASED ON THE COHERENCE PRINCIPLE

1. Guideline: Coherence effect: People learn better from multimedia messages when extraneous words, pictures, and sounds that are not directly relevant to the explanation are excluded rather than included.

2. Guideline based on: Research

3. Degree of confidence: High for short multimedia explanations of how something works.

4. Comments: The guideline is based on a collection of studies, including the following.

(1) Students read an illustrated text explaining how lightning storms develop. For some students, a few sentences were added that contained interesting stories and photos about lightning, such as what happened when a high school football player was struck by lightning (which can be called seductive details). Students who read the text that excluded interesting material performed better on subsequent transfer tests than did students whose text included additional interesting material.

(2) Students viewed a narrated animation explaining how lightning storms develop or how a car's braking system works. For some students, the presentation included background music and environmental sounds (such as the sound of metal grinding when the brakes went on). Students who viewed the animation with no music or sounds performed better on subsequent transfer tests than did students who viewed the animation that included music and sounds.

(3) Students viewed a narrated animation explaining how lightning storms develop. For some students, the presentation included several interspersed video segments depicting interesting events, such as a golfer being carried away after being struck by lightning (which can be called

seductive details). Students who viewed the animation without video clips performed better on subsequent transfer tests than did students who viewed the animation that included video clips.

5. References: Harp, S. F., & Mayer, R. E. (1998). How seductive details do their damage: A theory of cognitive interest in science learning. *Journal of Educational Psychology, 90,* 414–434.

Mayer, R. E., Bove, W., Bryman, A., Mars, R., & Tapangco, L. (1996). When less is more: Meaningful learning from visual and verbal summaries of science textbook lessons. *Journal of Educational Psychology, 88,* 64–78.

Mayer, R. E., Heiser, J., & Lonn, S. (2001). Cognitive constraints on multimedia learning: When presenting more material results in less understanding. *Journal of Educational Psychology, 93,* 187–198.

Moreno, R., & Mayer, R. E. (2000). A coherence effect in multimedia learning: The case for minimizing irrelevant sounds in the design of multimedia messages. *Journal of Educational Psychology, 92,* 117–125.

6. Glossary: **Seductive detail:** Interesting but extraneous material in a multimedia message (Harp & Mayer, 1998).

7. Users: Instructional designer, course manager, program manager

STRATEGIES BASED ON THE MODALITY PRINCIPLE

1. Guideline: Modality principle: People learn better from animation and verbal explanations in spoken form than from animation and onscreen text.

2. Guideline based on: Research

3. Degree of confidence: High for short multimedia explanations of how something works, how to carry out a procedure, or why an answer is incorrect.

4. Comments: The guideline is based on a collection of studies, including the following.

(1) Students were asked to view a short animation concerning how lightning storms develop, how a car's braking system works, or how a plant grows. Students who received concurrent narration performed better on subsequent transfer tests than did students who received concurrent onscreen text containing the same words as the narration.

(2) Students were given sheets showing the step-by-step solution of various geometry problems. Students who received concurrent taped-recorded speech explaining each step performed better on subsequent transfer tests than did students who received the same words printed on the sheets.

(3) Students explored the fuel system of a jet aircraft in a virtual reality environment and received an explanation of each part they visited. Students who received explanations of each part as narration performed better on subsequent transfer tests than did students who received the same explanations as printed text on a screen in the virtual environment.

5. References:

Mayer, R. E. (2001). *Multimedia learning.* Cambridge, UK: Cambridge University Press.

Moreno, R., & Mayer, R. E. (1999). Cognitive principles of multimedia learning: The role of modality and contiguity. *Journal of Educational Psychology, 91,* 358–368.

Moreno, R., Mayer, R. E., Spires, H. A., & Lester, J. C. (2001). The case for social agency in computer-based multimedia: Do students learn more deeply when they interact with animated pedagogical agents? *Cognition and Instruction, 19,* 177–214.

O'Neil, H. F., Jr., Mayer, R. E., Herl, H. E., Niemi, C., Olin, K., & Thurman, R. A. (2000). Instructional strategies for virtual aviation training environments. In H. F. O'Neil, Jr. & D. H. Andrews (Eds.), *Aircrew training and assessment* (pp. 105–130) Mahwah, NJ: Erlbaum.

6. Glossary: **Animation:** Moving pictures based on drawings (Mayer, 2001).

Explanation: A step-by-step description of how something works or a step-by-step description of how to carry out a procedure (Mayer, 2001).

Narration: Spoken text (Mayer, 2001).

Transfer: Using what was learned to solve new problems (Mayer, 2001).

7. Users: Instructional designer, course manager, program manager

STRATEGIES BASED ON THE MULTIMEDIA PRINCIPLE

1. Guideline: Multimedia principle: People learn better when presented with words and corresponding graphics (e.g., animation, video, illustrations, pictures) than from words alone.

2. Guideline based on: Research

3. Degree of confidence: High for short explanations of how something works or how to carry out a procedure.

4. Comments: The guideline is based on a collection of studies, including the following.

(1) Students listened to a short narration concerning how pumps or brakes work. For some students, a corresponding animation was presented depicting the actions described in the narration. Students who received both narration and animation performed better on transfer tests than students who received words alone.

(2) Students read text that explained how pumps work, how brakes work, how electrical generators work, or how lightning storms develop. For some students, a corresponding set of illustrations was presented with each frame depicting actions described in the text. Students who received both text and illustrations performed better than students who received text alone.

(3) Students were better able to learn about the laws of motion from a computer-based lesson that included animated graphics than one without graphics.

5. References:

Mayer, R. E. (2001). *Multimedia learning.* Cambridge, UK: Cambridge University Press.

Mayer, R. E., & Anderson, R. B. (1991). Animations need narrations: An experimental test of the dual-coding hypothesis. *Journal of Educational Psychology, 83,* 484–490.

Mayer, R. E., & Gallini, J. K. (1990). When is an illustration worth ten thousand words? *Journal of Educational Psychology, 82,* 715–726.

Rieber, L. (1990). Using computer generated graphics in science instruction. *Journal of Educational Psychology, 82,* 135–140.

6. Glossary: None

7. Users: Instructional designer, course manager, program manager

STRATEGIES BASED ON THE PERSONALIZATION PRINCIPLE

1. Guideline: Personalization principle: People learn a verbal explanation or a verbal description of a procedure better from multimedia lessons when the words are in conversational style (e.g., including first-person and second-person constructions) rather than formal style.

2. Guideline based on: Research

3. Degree of confidence:	Medium for short explanations of how something works or how to carry out a procedure.
4. Comments:	The guideline is based on a collection of studies, including the following.

(1) Students received a short, narrated animation explaining how lightning storms develop. For some students the narration was in formal style (e.g., using third-person constructions), whereas for other students the narration was in conversational style (e.g., using first- and second-person constructions). Students performed better on subsequent transfer tests when they had received conversational rather than formal narrations.

(2) Students learned how plants grow by viewing narrated animations within the context of an educational game. For some students, the narration was in formal style (e.g., using third-person constructions), whereas for other students, the narration was in conversational style (e.g., using first- and second-person constructions). Students performed better on subsequent transfer tests when they had received conversational rather than formal narrations.

5. References:	Mayer, R. E., & Moreno, R. (2002). Animation as an aid to multimedia learning. *Educational Psychology Review, 14,* 87–99.
	Moreno, R., & Mayer, R. E. (2000). Engaging students in active learning: The case for personalized multimedia messages. *Journal of Educational Psychology, 93,* 724–733.
	Symons, C. S., & Johnson, B. T. (1997). The self-reference effect in memory: A meta-analysis. *Psychological Bulletin, 121,* 371–394.
6. Glossary:	**Personalization:** Presenting words in conversational style rather than formal style (Moreno & Mayer, 2000).
7. Users:	Instructional designer, course manager, program manager

STRATEGIES BASED ON THE PRE-TRAINING PRINCIPLE

1. Guideline: Pre-training principle: People learn better from a multimedia presentation when they already know about the components in the presentation (i.e., prior to the presentation learners can visually recognize, name, and describe the behavior of each major component).

2. Guideline based on: Research

3. Degree of confidence: Medium for short explanations of how something works.

4. Comments: The guideline is based on a collection of studies, including the following.

(1) Students viewed a narrated animation depicting how a car's braking system works. Some students received pre-training in the location, name, and behavior of each component, for example, that the piston in the master cylinder could be forward or back. Students who received pre-training learned better from the multimedia explanation than those who received the same training after the presentation.

(2) Students viewed a narrated animation depicting how a tire pump works. Some students received pre-training in the location, name, and behavior of each component, for example, that the inlet valve could be open or closed. Students who received pre-training learned better from the multimedia explanation than those who did not.

5. References: Mayer, R. E., Mathias, A., & Wetzell, K. (2002). Fostering understanding of multimedia messages through pre-training: Evidence for a two-stage theory of mental model construction. *Journal of Experimental Psychology: Applied, 8,* 147–154.

Mayer, R. E., Mautone, P., & Prothero, W. (2002). Pictorial aids for learning by doing in a multimedia geology simulation game. *Journal of Educational Psychology, 94,* 171–185.

6. Glossary:	**Pre-training:** Prior to presenting a multimedia lesson, making sure that learners know about each component or element in the lesson (Mayer, Mathias, & Wetzell, 2002).
7. Users:	Instructional designer, course manager, program manager

STRATEGIES BASED ON PRIOR KNOWLEDGE PRINCIPLE

1. Guideline: Prior knowledge principle: Low prior knowledge learners benefit more from well-designed multimedia messages than do high prior knowledge learners.

2. Guideline based on: Research

3. Degree of confidence: Medium for short explanations of how something works.

4. Comments: The guideline is based on a collection of studies, including the following.

(1) Students received text and illustrations depicting how lightning storms develop. For some students, the text was presented near the corresponding graphic (integrated presentation), whereas for others, the text was presented far from the corresponding graphic (separated presentation). The positive effects of integrated presentation were strong for low prior knowledge learners but not for high prior knowledge learners.

(2) Students received text and illustrations explaining the operation of a bell-and-light circuit. For some students, the text was presented near the corresponding graphic (integrated presentation), whereas for others, the text was presented far from the corresponding graphic (separated presentation). The positive effects of inte-

grated presentation were strong for low prior knowledge learners but not for high prior knowledge learners.

5. References: Kalyuga, S., Chandler, P., & Sweller, J. (1998). Levels of expertise and instructional design. *Human Factors, 40,* 1–17.
Kalyuga, S., Chandler, P., & Sweller, J. (2000). Incorporating learner experience into the design of multimedia instruction. *Journal of Educational Psychology, 92,* 126–136.
Mayer, R. E. (2001). *Multimedia learning.* Cambridge, UK: Cambridge University Press.
Mayer, R. E., Steinhoff, K., Bower, G., & Mars, R. (1995). A generative theory of textbook design: Using annotated illustrations to foster meaningful learning of science text. *Educational Technology Research and Development, 43,* 31–43.

6. Glossary: None

7. Users: Instructional designer, course manager, program manager

STRATEGIES BASED ON THE REDUNDANCY PRINCIPLE

1. Guideline: Redundancy principle: People learn better from animation and narration than from animation, narration, and onscreen text (i.e., present verbal explanations solely in spoken form rather than in both spoken form and printed form).

2. Guideline based on: Research

3. Degree of confidence: High for short multimedia explanations of how something works or how to carry out a procedure.

4. Comments: The guideline is based on a collection of studies, including the following.

(1) Students were asked to view a short animation concerning how lightning storms develop along with corresponding narration. For some students, onscreen text was

presented at the bottom of the screen corresponding to the words in the narration. Students who viewed animations in which onscreen text was not added to the narrated animation performed better on subsequent transfer tests than students who viewed animations that included onscreen text.

(2) People learned how to solder metals in a computer-based program consisting of onscreen diagrams and accompanying narration. Some learners also received onscreen text that duplicated the words in the narration. Students learned better when onscreen text was not added to the narrated animation.

5. References:

Kalyuga, S., Chandler, P., & Sweller, J. (1999). Managing split-attention and redundancy in multimedia learning. *Applied Cognitive Psychology, 13,* 351–372.

Mayer, R. E., Heiser, J., & Lonn, S. (2001). Cognitive constraints on multimedia learning: When presenting more material results in less understanding. *Journal of Educational Psychology, 93,* 187–198.

Mayer, R. E., & Moreno, R. (2003). Nine ways to reduce cognitive load in multimedia learning. *Educational Psychologist, 38,* 43–52.

Moreno, R., & Mayer, R. E. (2002). Verbal redundancy in multimedia learning: When reading helps listening. *Journal of Educational Psychology, 94,* 156–163.

6. Glossary:

Redundancy: Presenting the same verbal message in printed and spoken form (Mayer & Moreno, 2003).

7. Users:

Instructional designer, course manager, program manager

STRATEGIES BASED ON THE SIGNALING PRINCIPLE

1. Guideline:

Signaling principle: People learn better from narrated animations when the narration highlights the key steps and the links between them (i.e., organize the narration to include a preview summary that outlines the main steps, section headings that correspond to the main steps, and pointer words such as *first, second, third,* or *as a result*).

2. Guideline based on: Research

3. Degree of confidence:

Medium for short explanations of how something works or descriptions of how to carry out a procedure.

4. Comments:

The guideline is based on a collection of studies, including the following.

(1) Students learned how airplanes achieve lift from a narrated animation. A signaled version included a preview summary outlining three main steps in the process, headings corresponding to the three steps, and pointer words such as *as a result*. Students who received the signaled version performed better on a transfer test than did students who received the nonsignaled version.

(2) Students read a passage about how the red tide happens. A signaled version included a preview summary outlining three main steps in the process, paragraph headings corresponding to these three steps, and pointer words such as *first, second,* or *third*. Students who received the signaled version performed better on a transfer test than did students who received the nonsignaled version.

5. References:

Loman, N. L., & Mayer, R. E. (1983). Signaling techniques that increase the understandability of expository prose. *Journal of Educational Psychology, 75,* 402–412.

Lorch, R. F., Jr. (1989). Text signaling devices and their effects on reading and memory

processes. *Educational Psychology Review, 1,*
209–234.

Mautone, P. D., & Mayer, R. E. (2001). Signaling
as a cognitive guide in multimedia learning.
Journal of Educational Psychology, 93, 377–389.

6. Glossary: **Signaling:** Adding a summary preview that outlines the steps in a process or explanation, head-
ings that correspond to the steps, and pointer
words such as *first, second,* or *third* (Mautone &
Mayer, 2001).

7. Users: Instructional designer, course manager, program manager

STRATEGIES BASED ON THE SPATIAL CONTIGUITY PRINCIPLE

1. Guideline: Spatial contiguity principle: People learn better
when corresponding words and graphics are
placed near rather than far from each other on
the screen (i.e., place each set of printed words
near rather than far from the portion of the
graphic they describe).

2. Guideline based on: Research

3. Degree of confidence: High for short multimedia explanations of how
something works.

4. Comments: The guideline is based on a collection of studies,
including the following.

(1) Students viewed an animation depicting
how lightning storms develop. Corresponding on-screen text was placed either at the
bottom of the frame as a caption (separated
presentation) or next to the portion of the
animation that it described (integrated presentation). Students who received the integrated presentation performed better on
transfer tests than did students who
received the separated presentation.

(2) Students read a text with illustrations
explaining how lightning storms develop or

how a car's braking system works. The text was placed either on a separate page (separated presentation) or next to the portion of the illustration that it described (integrated presentation). Students who received the integrated presentation performed better on transfer tests than did students who received the separated presentation.

(3) Students received instruction in how to solve geometry problems that included graphics and text. The text was placed either on a separate page (separated presentation) or next to the portion of the illustration that it described (integrated presentation). Students who received the integrated presentation performed better on transfer tests than did students who received the separated presentation, presumably because the integrated presentation eliminates *split attention*.

5. References:

Mayer, R. E., & Moreno, R. (2003). Nine ways to reduce cognitive load in multimedia learning. *Educational Psychologist, 38,* 43–52.

Mayer, R. E., Steinhoff, K., Bower, G., & Mars, R. (1995). A generative theory of textbook design: Using annotated illustrations to foster meaningful learning of science text. *Educational Technology Research and Development, 43,* 31–43.

Moreno, R., & Mayer, R. E. (1999). Cognitive principles of multimedia learning: The role of modality and contiguity. *Journal of Educational Psychology, 91,* 358–368.

Sweller, J., Chandler, P., Tierney, P., & Cooper, M. (1990). Cognitive load as a factor in the structuring of technical material. *Journal of Experimental Psychology: General, 119,* 176–192.

6. Glossary:

Split attention presentations: Multimedia presentations in which corresponding words and

graphics are not placed near each other
(Sweller, Chandler, Tierney, & Cooper, 1990).

7. Users: Instructional designer, course manager, program manager

STRATEGIES BASED ON THE TEMPORAL CONTIGUITY PRINCIPLE

1. Guideline: Temporal contiguity principle: People learn better when corresponding animation and narra-
tion segments are presented at the same time.

2. Guideline based on: Research

3. Degree of confidence: High for short multimedia explanations of how
something works or how to carry out a procedure.

4. Comments: The guideline is based on a collection of studies,
including the following.

(1) Students viewed a short animation depicting how a pump works, how the human
lungs work, how a car's braking system
works, or how lightning storms develop.
Corresponding narration was presented
either simultaneously with the animation,
after the animation, or before the animation. When animation and corresponding
narration were presented simultaneously,
students performed better on subsequent
transfer tests.

(2) Students watched a film showing how to
assemble some parts from a kit. Students
who viewed the film in which the film
soundtrack corresponded to actions being
depicted in the film performed better on
transfer tests than did students who viewed
the film in which the soundtrack either preceded or followed the corresponding visual
material by 14 seconds or more.

5. References: Baggett, P. (1984). Role of temporal overlap of
visual and auditory material in forming dual

media associations. *Journal of Educational Psychology, 76,* 408–417.

Mayer, R. E., & Anderson, R. B. (1991). Animations need narrations: An experimental test of a dual-coding hypothesis. *Journal of Educational Psychology, 83,* 484–490.

Mayer, R. E., & Moreno, R. (2003). Nine ways to reduce cognitive load in multimedia learning. *Educational Psychologist, 38,* 43–52.

Mayer, R. E., Moreno, R., Boire, M., & Vagge, S. (1999). Maximizing constructivist learning from multimedia communications by minimizing cognitive load. *Journal of Educational Psychology, 91,* 638–643.

6. Glossary: None

7. Users: Instructional designer, course manager, program manager

STRATEGIES BASED ON THE VOICE PRINCIPLE

1. Guideline: Voice principle: People learn better from narrated animations when the narration has a human voice with a standard accent rather than a machine voice or an accented voice.

2. Guideline based on: Research

3. Degree of confidence: Medium for short explanations of how something works or descriptions of how to carry out a procedure.

4. Comments: The guideline is based on a collection of studies, including the following.

(1) Students listened to a short narrated animation concerning how lightning storms develop. Students who listened to a narration consisting of a human voice performed better on subsequent transfer tests than did students who listened to a narration consisting of a machine-simulated voice.

(2) Students listened to a short narrated animation concerning how lightning storms

develop. Students who listened to a narration consisting of a human voice with a standard accent performed better on subsequent transfer tests than did students who listened to a narration consisting of a human voice with a foreign accent.

5. References: Mayer, R. E., & Moreno, R. (2003). Nine ways to reduce cognitive load in multimedia learning. *Educational Psychologist, 38,* 43–52.
Mayer, R. E., Sobko, K., & Mautone, P. D. (2003). Social cues in multimedia learning: Role of speaker's voice. *Journal of Educational Psychology, 95,* 419–425.
Oviatt, S., & Adams, B. (2000). Designing and evaluating conversational interfaces with animated characters. In J. Cassell, J. Sullivan, S. Prevost, & E. Churchill (Eds.), *Embodied conversational agents* (pp. 319–345). Cambridge, MA: MIT Press.

6. Glossary: None

7. Users: Instructional designer, course manager, program manager

CHAPTER 3

INSTRUCTIONAL STRATEGIES

Richard Clark
University of Southern California

The following guidelines are presented in this chapter:

Strategies Based on Providing Learner Control of Instructional Navigation
Strategies Based on Providing Worked Examples and Practice
Strategies Based on Effective Feedback during Learning
Strategies Based on Teaching Concepts
Strategies Based on Teaching Process Knowledge
Strategies Based on Teaching Causal Principles
Strategies Based on Teaching Procedural ("How to") Knowledge

STRATEGIES BASED ON PROVIDING LEARNER CONTROL OF INSTRUCTIONAL NAVIGATION

1. Guideline:	As the extent of learner control increases, learning decreases except for the most advanced expert learners.
2. Guideline based on:	Research

What Works in Distance Learning: Guidlines, pages 25–39
Copyright © 2005 by Information Age Publishing
All rights of reproduction in any form reserved.

3. Degree of confidence: High

4. Comments: The high levels of learner control afforded by distance learning media and contexts are often described as one of the potential advantages of distance learning (Hannafin & Sullivan, 1995). Yet the evidence from a great variety of studies examining different learners, learning tasks, and settings suggests that as the extent of learner control over various aspects of instruction increases, learning may decrease. This seems to be the case even when learners are assigned to their preferred level of control over instructional presentations (Niemiec, Sikorski, & Walberg, 1996).

While it is possible to find studies that provide evidence for the benefits of some limited forms of learner control, such as control over the pacing of a presentation (Doherty, 1998), it is likely that more extensive control aids only the learning of students with very high levels of prior knowledge of the subject matter and/or those who have learned how to benefit from increased control. A comprehensive review and meta-analysis of many learner control studies by Niemiec and colleagues (1996) reported an overall negative impact. This negative impact extends to studies where learners were allowed to select the amount of control they exercised over their course (Hannifin & Sullivan, 1995). While system control of instructional events and strategies may not be helpful to more advanced students, it apparently does not harm them (Hannifin & Sullivan, 1995). Thus it does not appear to be harmful to provide system control of instruction to more advanced learners.

5. References: Doherty, P. D. (1998). Learner control in asynchronous learning environments. *ALN Magazine, 2*(2). Retrieved December 4, 2002, from http://www.aln.org/alnweb/magazine/vol2_issue2/doherty.htm#1-7

Hannafin, R. D., & Sullivan, H. D. (1995). Learner control in full and lean CAI programs. *Educational Technology Research and Development, 43*(3), 19–30.

Niemiec, R. P., Sikorski, C., & Walberg, H. J. (1996). Learner-control effects: A review of reviews and a meta-analysis. *Journal of Educational Computing Research, 15,* 157–174.

6. Glossary:

Contingencies: Decision rules that guide instructional presentations based on learner performance within a course. For example, if a learner enters a wrong answer for a practice test item, a system contingency might be to direct the student to review relevant sections of the lesson and then repeat the practice.

Instructional strategies: Methods of organizing, sequencing, and presenting instruction that increase both student learning and the transfer of their learning to application contexts. Instructional strategies or methods are external representations of internal cognitive processes that are required to learn but which learners will not or cannot provide for themselves efficiently or effectively.

Learner control: The degree to which instruction permits individual students to control the path, pace, and/or contingencies of instruction.

Learning strategies: The techniques or methods students use to learn or acquire new information. Learning strategies are methods used by learners to learn; instructional strategies are methods that the instructional program provides to support learning.

Pacing: The speed with which a course presents information to students.

Sequencing: The order in which information, lessons, and learning tasks are presented to students within a course.

7. Users:

Instructional designer and developer

STRATEGIES BASED ON PROVIDING WORKED EXAMPLES AND PRACTICE

1. Guideline: When instruction provides clear and complete procedural "worked" examples of the decisions and actions needed to solve problems and perform necessary tasks to be learned, then learning and transfer to work performance will be increased.

2. Guideline based on: Research

3. Degree of confidence: High

4. Comments: Experiments comparing worked examples with conceptual instruction and problem-based discovery learning (Kalyuga, Chandler, Touvinen, & Sweller, 2001; Touvinen & Sweller, 1999) found clear evidence that worked examples were superior and enhanced not only learning but transfer of learning outside of the training setting. Touvinen and Sweller (1999) and Kalyuga and colleagues (2001) also found that the benefit of worked examples decreased and the benefit of problem solving increased as learners became more expert. Van Merrienböer (1997) strongly suggested that the use of worked examples to solve task-relevant problems should be an essential component of all practice during instruction (with accompanying conceptual explanations of why different elements of the procedure "work" to achieve a performance goal). These worked examples should also result from a cognitive task analysis.

Touvinen and Sweller (1999) demonstrated that when properly designed, worked examples are superior to discovery learning for all but the most advanced learners, and that even advanced experts get equal benefit from discovery learning and worked examples and so seem not to be harmed by examples. However, Kalyuga and colleagues (2001) found that experts benefited more from solving problems than from worked examples. van Merrienböer, Clark, and de Croock (2002) provided an example of a worked example for teaching Web-based information search.

5. References:

Kalyuga, S., Chandler, P., Touvinen, J., & Sweller, J. (2001). When problem solving is superior to worked examples. *Journal of Educational Psychology, 93,* 579–588.

Touvinen, J. E., & Sweller, J. (1999). A comparison of cognitive load associated with discovery learning and worked examples. *Journal of Educational Psychology, 91,* 334–341.

van Merrienböer, J. J. G. (1997). *Training complex cognitive skills: A four-component instructional design model for technical training.* Englewood Cliffs, NJ: Educational Technology Publications.

van Merrienböer, J. J. G., Clark, R. E., & de Croock, B. M. (2002). Blueprints for complex learning: The 4C/ID-model. *Educational Technology Research and Development, 50*(2), 39–64.

6. Glossary:

Cognitive task analysis: A method of analyzing decision and analytical procedures in which an interviewer collects from experts a temporal order of overt actions and mental (covert) decisions (solutions) required to achieve a goal state from a given state (problem or current conditions).

Given state: The description of an existing problem or current "condition" that must be changed in order to achieve a "goal state" or objective.

Goal state: The desired end-result or objective of the performance being learned.

Procedure: A sequenced list of overt actions and covert decisions (with the criteria or rules for selecting alternatives as decisions are being made) that enables the learner to transform a given state to a goal state.

7. User:

Instructional designer

STRATEGIES BASED ON EFFECTIVE FEEDBACK DURING LEARNING

1. Guideline: The more that learning and performance feedback (a) is based on concrete learning goals that are clearly understood by students, (b) describes the gap between the student's learning goal and the student's current performance and suggests how to close that gap, and (c) focuses the student's attention on the learning goal and not on his/her failure to achieve the goal, the more effective it becomes for learners, learning, and transfer of learning to performance settings.

2. Guideline based on: Research

3. Degree of confidence: High

4. Comments: Feedback during learning has been examined for many years by many different researchers with very mixed and often conflicting results (Kluger & DiNisi, 1998). Recent attempts to resolve these disagreements have begun to pay off. For example, a recent international review of well-designed performance feedback research studies (Kluger & DiNisi, 1998) produced a surprising insight. Performance feedback actually depressed performance in one-third of all feedback research studies conducted both in natural settings and in the laboratory. In another third of the studies, performance feedback had no impact. In only one-third of the studies did feedback increase performance.

It appears that effective performance feedback must be focused on building the learner's self-efficacy for the learning task and closing the gap between learning and/or performance goals and the individual's current progress. Feedback is effective only when learning goals are clearly understood. When feedback points out poor performance or a lack of performance, or when it suggests that the performer is "wrong" or is being made responsible for goals that were not made clear initially, performance most often deteriorates. This finding by Kluger and DiNisi reflects a similar conclusion reached as a result of two very solid but independent research programs directed by Bandura and Locke (2003), who argued that "discrepancy" feedback often damages both learning and performance. They explained that making a person responsible for mistakes not only restricts current learning but often damages future learning by impacting self-efficacy. Kluger and DiNisi also emphasized that when adults feel that their learning will be directly transferable to their work and when their work performance is connected to their personal growth, performance feedback is most beneficial. The finding that poor feedback was obvious in two-thirds of all the research studies in Kluger and DiNisi's review suggests that it may be even more prevalent in practice since researchers tend to select what are thought to be the best strategies to test in experiments. Thus the best feedback appears to involve complimentary comments about what was done well and a dialogue about strategies for achieving goals that are not yet attained.

It is doubtful that any feedback strategy will work equally well for all learners or that a strategy that conforms to the suggestions made by Kluger and DiNisi (1998) will succeed for everyone. There is some evidence, for example, that learners who are motivated to "look good" but who do not value learning what is being taught will not benefit from learning results or strategy feedback, and there is also evidence that when learning tasks are easy to achieve, pointing out mistakes and attributing them to the learner may be helpful (Wofford & Goodwin, 1990).

5. References:

Bandura, A., & Locke, E. A. (2003). Negative self-efficacy and goal effects revisited. *Journal of Applied Psychology, 88,* 87–99.

Kluger, A., & DiNisi, A. (1998). Feedback interventions: Toward the understanding of a double-edged sword. *Current Directions in Psychological Science,* 7(3), 67–72.

Wofford, J. C., & Goodwin, V. L. (1990). Effects of feedback on cognitive processing and choice of decision style. *Journal of Applied Psychology,* 75, 603–612.

6. Glossary: **Discrepancy feedback:** A negative feedback control system aimed at error correction (Bandura & Locke, 2003).

7. User: Instructional designer

STRATEGIES BASED ON TEACHING CONCEPTS

1. Guideline: If new concepts are taught by providing a definition of the concept, examples from the work environment, and practice exercises in which learners are asked to correctly classify many different work-relevant concept examples, then learning will be enhanced.

2. Guideline based on: Research

3. Degree of confidence: High

4. Comments: Concepts are any unit of knowledge that has a definition and at least one example. Students must often learn a great variety of concepts to support accurate classification of events and objects in their work environment. When designing instruction for concepts, it is vital to begin by developing an accurate definition that contains a complete list of only the defining attributes or features of the concept. In addition, instruction must provide work-related examples and practice exercises in which learners are asked to classify a number of new examples of the concepts being learned. This type of instruction results in learning that should transfer to work environments or out of the classroom to everyday life (Howard, 2000).

   If transfer is required to very novel applications beyond the current work environment (far transfer), then in addition to practice classifying work-related examples, instructional designers should also include a variety of novel examples of each concept. The more that learners practice classifying varied and novel examples, the higher the probability that they will be able classify very novel new examples in a variety of contexts (Howard, 2000).

5. References: Howard, R. W. (2000). Generalization and transfer: An interrelation of paradigms and a taxonomy of knowledge extension processes. *Review of General Psychology, 4,* 211–237.

Merrill, M. D. (1983). Component display theory. In C. M. Reigeluth (Ed.), *Instructional design theories and models: An overview of their current status* (pp. 279–333). Hillsdale, NJ: Erlbaum.

Merrill, M. D., & Tennyson, R. D. (1977). *Teaching concepts: An instructional design guide.* Englewood Cliffs, NJ: Educational Technology Publications.

6. Glossary: **Concepts:** Any unit of knowledge that has a definition and at least one example.

Far transfer: Knowledge is generalized from the context and examples where it was originally learned and is applied to contexts and examples that are extraordinarily different from the original learning context.

Near transfer: Knowledge is generalized from the context and examples where it was originally learned and is applied to contexts and examples that exist in a work environment that is similar to the one emphasized during learning.

7. User: Instructional designer

STRATEGIES BASED ON TEACHING PROCESS KNOWLEDGE

1. Guideline: When designing instruction for a process (how something works), give students a clear narrative description integrated with a visual model of the sequence of events that characterize the process, and describe each stage in the process and what key events or actions occur at each stage to produce a change that leads to the next stage.

2. Guideline based on: Research

3. Degree of confidence: Medium

4. Comments:

Learning about processes (how something works) requires that a student be able to accurately describe each stage in the process, the actions that occur at each stage, and how the consequences of each action lead to the next stage. Designers sometimes confuse processes with procedures (how someone does something). Processes are often called "mental models" in instructional research. Visual models of a process are often accompanied by a fully integrated narrative of events that occur at each stage and how they lead to the next stage to help students remember both the sequence of stages and the events that occur at each stage.

Process knowledge helps learners develop a mental model of an important series of related events in a work setting. Processes can, for example, describe human activities (how a team functions, or should function, to achieve a task), biological events (photosynthesis), or mechanical systems (how the expended shell rejection mechanism works on a weapon). It is important to remember that learning about a process will not ensure that learners will be able to use the process to, for example, make accurate predictions or engage in troubleshooting. Both prediction ("What if . . .?") and troubleshooting ("Here is a problem with the system . . . fix it") require procedural knowledge, worked examples, and a great deal of practice (learn by doing).

5. References:

Carroll, J., & Olson, J. (1988). Mental models in human–computer interaction. In M. Helander (Ed.), *Handbook of human–computer interaction* (pp. 45–65). Amsterdam: North-Holland.

Markman, A., & Gentner, D. (2000). Thinking. *Annual Review of Psychology, 52,* 223–247.

Merrill, M. D. (1983). Component display theory. In C. M. Reigeluth (Ed.), *Instructional design theories and models: An overview of their current status* (pp. 279–333). Hillsdale, NJ: Erlbaum.

Merrill, M. D. (2000). Knowledge objects and mental models. In D. Wiley (Ed.), *The instructional use of learning objects.* Bloomington, IN: AIT/AECT. Retrieved October 17, 2002, from http://www.reusability.org/read/chapters/merrill.doc

6. Glossary: **Mental model:** "A representation (in our mind) of a physical or biological or social system, with a plausible cascade of causal associations connecting the input to the output. In other words, the mental model is a mental structure that reflects the user's understanding of a system" (Carroll & Olson, 1988, p. 34).

Process knowledge: Knowledge about how something works. "It answers the question, 'What happens?' " (Merrill, 2000, p. 12).

Worked example: A description of "how to," providing clear, step-by-step descriptions of all actions and decisions necessary to achieve a performance goal in the context of a demonstration of an application to a typical problem in a setting that mirrors the application environment where the procedure will be used.

7. User: Instructional designer

STRATEGIES BASED ON TEACHING CAUSAL PRINCIPLES

1. Guideline: When teaching causal principles, the more the learner is provided (a) a statement about the cause and resulting effects, (b) a worked example drawn from the application setting, (c) practice that encourages the elaboration of the elements and sequence of the causal chain and then application of the principle to solve a problem that requires a prediction, and (d) practice in the application of the principle to gradually more novel and complex examples, the more effective will be the learning and transfer to the job.

2. Guideline based on: Research

3. Degree of confidence: Medium

4. Comments: Effective training often requires that learners understand the conceptual or scientific basis for work processes and procedures. Causal principles reflect the content of some of the most complex knowledge background for technical procedures. Reigeluth (1999) described the many different instructional strategies that have been found to help learners acquire knowledge about causal principles. He suggested first defining the cause–effect relationship (a generality) and then providing a typical worked example. To achieve maximum learner participation, Reigeluth suggested providing opportunities to explore a dynamic example. For instance, in a distance, computer-based lesson on the principles that influence the behavior of light on different types of lenses, the learner might be invited to click on tabs that change the thickness or shape of a lens (cause) and see the path, focal distance, and magnification of the image (effects) change correspondingly.

During instruction, it seems more effective to focus the learner's attention on important elements of the principle and suggest shorthand ways to describe it. Examples and practice exercises should begin with simple worked examples and then gradually present more complex, novel, and difficult examples in which learners are asked first to describe and label each phase of the cause-and-effect chain in the correct order, and then, when given one phase, to predict the next phase or the previous phase, and

then to use the principle to solve increasingly
novel problems.

5. References: Merrill, M. D. (1983). Component display theory. In C. M. Reigeluth (Ed.), *Instructional
design theories and models: An overview of their
current status* (pp. 279–333). Hillsdale, NJ:
Erlbaum.

Newton, D. E. (1996). Causal situations in science: A model for supporting understanding. *Learning and Instruction, 6,* 201–217.

Reigeluth, C. M. (1999). *Instructional-design theories and models: Volume II.* Mahwah, NJ:
Erlbaum. [See chapter on teaching principles.] Summarized and retrieved December
4, 2002, from http://www.indiana.edu/
~idtheory/methods/module_5_4.html

6. Glossary: **Worked example:** A description of "how to," providing clear, step-by-step descriptions of all
actions and decisions necessary to achieve a
performance goal in the context of a demonstration of an application to a typical
problem in a setting that mirrors the application environment where the procedure
will be used.

7. User: Instructional designer

STRATEGIES BASED ON TEACHING PROCEDURAL ("HOW TO") KNOWLEDGE

1. Guideline: Effective instruction about "how to" procedures
should provide (a) clear, step-by-step "how to"
descriptions of all actions and decisions necessary to achieve a performance goal,
(b) demonstration of the procedure with a
model and/or worked example, (c) conceptual
knowledge in the form of concepts, processes,
and principles that explain why the procedure
works, and (d) the opportunity to practice the
procedure on problems and in settings that mir-

ror the application environment where the procedure will be used.

2. Guideline based on: Research

3. Degree of confidence: High

4. Comments: "The ultimate aim of training is procedural learning, that is, for trainees to be competent in performing a job" (Druckman & Bjork, 1994, p. 147). Thus learners must be able to translate all instruction into step-by-step actions and decisions, transfer them from training, and apply them appropriately on the job to achieve performance goals. Instructional strategies for teaching procedures require the development of an accurate and clearly described sequence of necessary actions and decisions. Procedures that are derived from expert-based cognitive task analysis (van Merrienböer, Clark, & de Croock, 2002) are preferable.

When teaching procedures, the more that instruction is based on expert-based descriptions of the sequence of actions and decisions necessary for goal achievement, and is accompanied by one or more worked examples and the opportunity for part–whole practice that reflects the learner's prior knowledge, and is accompanied by a conceptual elaboration of the declarative knowledge base supporting the procedure, the more effective will be the learning and transfer of the procedure back to the job environment.

Elaborate expert procedures should be chunked into segments of seven to nine new (to the learner) steps (to avoid cognitive overload) during instruction and accompanied by worked examples and conceptual explanations of their underlying principles, processes, and concepts. Where possible, practice of team-based procedures should occur in cooperative groups. When practicing, learners should be asked to explain orally or in writing how a solution was achieved. Practice of parts of a procedure must be followed by "whole task" practice where procedural chunks are gradually assembled into larger "wholes," and feedback should focus on closing the gap between current and required performance (Druckman & Bjork, 1994).

5. References:

Clark, R. E. (1999). Yin and yang cognitive motivational processes operating in multimedia learning environments. In J. J. G. van Merrienböer (Ed.), *Cognition and multimedia design* (pp. 73–107). Herleen, Netherlands: Open University Press.

Druckman, D., & Bjork, R. A. (1994). *Learning, remembering, believing: Enhancing human performance.* Washington, DC: National Academy Press.

Merrill, M. D. (1983). Component display theory. In C. M. Reigeluth (Ed.), *Instructional design theories and models: An overview of their current status* (pp. 279–333). Hillsdale, NJ: Erlbaum.

van Merrienböer, J. J. G., Clark, R. E., & de Croock, B. M. (2002). Blueprints for complex learning: The 4C/ID-model. *Educational Technology Research and Development, 50*(2), 39–64.

6. Glossary:

Cognitive overload: A condition where the amount of declarative information that a learner is attempting to hold in working memory (consciousness) in order to learn or solve problems exceeds its capacity (estimated to be 4 +/– 1 chunk of declarative knowledge). Overload is hypothesized to result in a shifting of attention away from learning goals (Clark, 1999).

Worked example: A description of "how to," providing clear, step-by-step descriptions of all actions and decisions necessary to achieve a performance goal in the context of a demonstration of an application to a typical problem in a setting that mirrors the application environment where the procedure will be used.

7. User:

Instructional designer

CHAPTER 4

LEARNING STRATEGIES

Myron H. Dembo and Linda Gubler Junge
University of Southern California

The following guidelines are presented in this chapter:

Strategies Based on Text Summarization
Strategies Based on Annotation
Strategies Based on Visual Representations
Strategies Based on Elaborative Interrogation
Strategies Based on Elaborative Verbal Rehearsal
Strategies Based on Generation of Higher Level Questions
Strategies Based on Outline-Formatted Notes
Strategies Based on Test Preparation
Strategies Based on Help Seeking
Strategies Based on Time Management
Strategies Based on Goal Setting
Strategies Based on Test Anxiety Reduction

What Works in Distance Learning: Guidlines, pages 41–63
Copyright © 2005 by Information Age Publishing
All rights of reproduction in any form reserved.

STRATEGIES BASED ON TEXT SUMMARIZATION

1. Guideline: Students who summarize readings comprehend and recall more than students who do not.

2. Guideline based on: Research

3. Degree of confidence: High

4. Comments: The process of summarizing text after reading provides students the opportunity to both generate meaning and monitor understanding. When summarizing, students make connections between words, sentences, paragraphs, and concepts in the text in addition to making connections to personal knowledge and experience; through this process, personal meaning is generated and ideas are elaborated on as they are organized in essay form (Wittrock, 1990). This generative process that requires elaboration and organization facilitates the process of depositing information into long-term memory for later recall (King, 1992). Summarization activities direct attention to academic tasks and allow students to monitor what they do and do not understand. They are prepared to review concepts and reread as necessary. Summarizing text is also beneficial in the test preparation process because students must adequately comprehend the material in order to put it into their own words.

Students in distance learning settings work independently, without the direct assistance of peers and/or instructors. Therefore, it is important that they be able to monitor their own learning, elaborate upon it, and organize it in order to recall it later and improve comprehension.

5. References: Dembo, M. (2004). *Motivation and learning strategies for college success* (2nd ed.). Mahwah, NJ: Erlbaum.

King, A. (1992). Comparison of self-questioning, summarizing, and note taking review as strategies for learning from lectures. *American Educational Research Journal, 29,* 303–323.

Simpson, M., & Nist, S. (2000). An update on strategic learning: It's more than textbook reading strategies. *Journal of Adolescent and Adult Literacy, 43,* 528–542.

Wittrock, M. C. (1990). Generative processes of comprehension. *Educational Psychologist, 24,* 345–376.

6. Glossary: **Elaboration:** Integrating meaningful knowledge into long-term memory through adding detail, summarizing, and creating examples and analogies (Dembo, 2004).

Generative process: The construction of meaning by building relations among the parts of the text and between the text and personal knowledge and experience (Wittrock, 1990).

Summarization: Condensing the main points of a text into one's own words (Wittrock, 1990).

7. User: Instructional designer

STRATEGIES BASED ON ANNOTATION

1. Guideline: Annotating text while reading improves comprehension.

2. Guideline based on: Research

3. Degree of confidence: High

4. Comments: Annotation takes less time than traditional strategies like rereading, outlining, and taking notes, and it is more useful than highlighting because it is an active, not a passive, process. It requires connecting to prior knowledge and experiences, as well as elaboration of ideas. When students annotate a text, they actively interact with it much as they would when conversing with another individual. It is important that students focus on ideas in annotations instead of topics. Perhaps the greatest selling point of annotation is that it naturally lends itself to test preparation activities and review. Students do not have to begin test preparation by distinguishing what is important from what is not important. This was done during the annotation process, as were generating potential test questions and identifying concepts that were not understood.

Annotation proves especially valuable when students find themselves isolated in a distance learning environment. This process aids them in finding the main point and guides understanding in an interactive way.

5. References: Dembo, M. (2004). *Motivation and learning strategies for college success* (2nd ed.). Mahwah, NJ: Erlbaum.

Nist, S., & Hogrebe, M. (1987). The role of underlining and annotating in remembering textual information. *Reading Research and Instruction, 27*(1), 12–25.

Nist, S., & Holschuh, J. (2000). Comprehension strategies at the college level. In R. F. Flippo & D. C. Caverly (Eds.), *Handbook of college reading and study strategy research* (pp. 75–104). Mahwah, NJ: Erlbaum.

Simpson, M., & Nist, S. (1990). Textbook annotation: An effective and efficient study strategy for college students. *Journal of Reading, 34*, 122–129.

6. Glossary: **Annotate:** To state key ideas briefly in one's own words in the margins of the text; and/or to enumerate multiple ideas (i.e., causes, effects, characteristics) in an organized fashion; and/or to note examples of concepts in the margin by writing EX; and/or to put key information on graphs and charts with the text when appropriate; and/or to jot down possible test questions; and/or to note puzzling or confusing ideas with a question mark in the margin; and/or to selectively underline key words or phrases (Simpson & Nist, 1990).

Elaboration: Integrating meaningful knowledge into long-term memory through adding detail, summarizing, and creating examples and analogies (Dembo, 2004).

7. User: Instructional designer

STRATEGIES BASED ON VISUAL REPRESENTATIONS

1. Guideline: Visual representation of text material is helpful in improving comprehension of complex material.

2. Guideline based on: Research

3. Degree of confidence: Medium

4. Comments: Reading involves two processes: comprehension and retention. Just because textbook material is comprehended does not mean that it will be retained. Additional steps such as visual representations improve comprehension of detailed material, and also improve retention and performance. When students are left primarily to themselves to read, comprehend, and retain material, as is the case in distance learning settings, visual representations are especially helpful, once students have been trained in when and how to use them.

Visual representations come with a variety of names and formats—graphic organizers, concept maps, hierarchies, matrices, flow charts, and so on. It is generally believed that in order to gain maximum benefit from employing visual representations, a training period on when and how to use them is necessary. Visual representations are most helpful when produced after reading because the students then have the information to represent and organize. Visually representing materials requires students to spend additional time with the content, going more in depth with it as a representation is generated. This additional time allows opportunity for the synthesis of concepts and the clarification of relationships when dealing with complex material. This process could be especially helpful if multiple texts are involved because the material can be brought together and synthesized in one visual representation that shows how the content is interrelated.

5. References: Bernard, R., & Naidu, S. (1992). Post-questioning, concept mapping and feedback: A distance education field experiment. *British Journal of Educational Technology, 23,* 48–60.

Dembo, M. (2004). *Motivation and learning strategies for college success* (2nd ed.). Mahwah, NJ: Erlbaum.

Moore, D., & Readence, J. (1984). A quantitative and qualitative review of graphic organizer research. *Journal of Educational Research, 78,* 11–17.

Nist, S., & Holschuh, J. (2000). Comprehension strategies at the college level. In R. F. Flippo & D. C. Caverly (Eds.), *Handbook of college reading and study strategy research* (pp. 75–104). Mahwah, NJ: Erlbaum.

6. Glossary:

Concept map: Any visual representation of a concept, theory, or information (Bernard & Naidu, 1992).

Elaboration: Integration of meaningful knowledge into long-term memory through adding detail, summarizing, and creating examples and analogies (Dembo, 2004).

Hierarchy: An organization of ideas into levels and groups (Dembo, 2004).

Matrix: An organization that displays the comparative relations existing within and across topics (Dembo, 2004).

7. User:

Instructional designer

STRATEGIES BASED ON ELABORATIVE INTERROGATION

1. Guideline:

Students who interact with texts by forming and answering questions based on readings show greater comprehension.

2. Guideline based on:

Research

3. Degree of confidence:

High

4. Comments:

Elaborative interrogation means that students interact with a text by forming and answering questions based on the reading, thereby turning what was a passive reading process into an active one. Knowledge is actively constructed as questions are formed, as relations between concepts are clarified, and as prior knowledge is accessed to answer questions. Engaging prior knowledge is key in gaining meaningful understanding that relates to what students already know and have experienced.

One elaborative interrogation strategy that helps students monitor comprehension and focus attention is to turn text headings and subheadings into questions. For example, if "The Industrial Revolution" was a textbook heading in an economics book, it would be turned into a question like "What was the impact of the Industrial Revolution on the world economy?" This activity prepares students to identify the main point of a passage, a task that many adults do not do effectively (Pressley, Symons, McDaniel, Snyder, & Turnure, 1988).

Another elaborative interrogation strategy that positively impacts learning is for learners to continually ask "why," "what," or "how" questions in their minds during reading. This process allows students to focus their attention, to monitor what is being understood, and to see where there may be gaps in comprehension. It also provides opportunity for further elaboration of ideas (extensions, inferences, etc.).

Distance learners need to use effective learning strategies such as elaborative interrogation if they are to succeed in their autonomous setting. Students are prone to miss key ideas without an instructor present to answer questions and clarify main points. Elaborative interrogation guides students' attention so that they will not miss the main points of the content.

5. References:

Dembo, M. (2004). *Motivation and learning strategies for college success* (2nd ed.). Mahwah, NJ: Erlbaum.

Nist, S., & Holschuh, J. (2000). Comprehension strategies at the college level. In R. F. Flippo & D. C. Caverly (Eds.), *Handbook of college reading and study strategy research* (pp. 75–104). Mahwah, NJ: Erlbaum.

Pressley, M., Ghatala, E., Woloshyn, V., & Pirie, J. (1990). Sometimes adults miss the main ideas and do not realize it: Confidence in responses to short-answer and multiple-choice comprehension questions. *Reading Research Quarterly, 25,* 232–249.

Pressley, M., Symons, S., McDaniel, M., Snyder, B., & Turnure, J. (1988). Elaborative interrogation facilitates acquisition of confusing facts. *Journal of Educational Psychology, 80,* 268–278.

Rosenshine, B., Meister, C., & Chapman, S. (1996). Teaching students to generate questions: A review of the intervention studies. *Review of Educational Research, 66,* 181–221.

6. Glossary:

Elaboration: Integrating meaningful knowledge into long-term memory through adding detail, summarizing, and creating examples and analogies (Dembo, 2004).

Interrogation: The process through which questions are generated and answered (Pressley et al., 1988).

7. User:

Instructional designer

STRATEGIES BASED ON ELABORATIVE VERBAL REHEARSAL

1. Guideline:

When students explain a concept or idea out loud, either to another person or an imaginary audience, their comprehension improves.

2. Guideline based on: Research

3. Degree of confidence: High

4. Comments:

The idea that the teacher often learns more than the students is embodied in the elaborative verbal rehearsal strategy, wherein students verbally explain, either to another person or an imagined audience, material that was learned in a lecture or in a reading assignment. Generalizations are constructed, personal examples are provided, and applications are offered as the information is verbally rehearsed. In this way students move away from less meaningful rote learning and are able to elaborate on the learned information, making it meaningful. They also become aware of what is not well understood and are thus prepared to reread, ask questions, and seek help as necessary.

For example, a student preparing for a test on material about the Industrial Revolution would verbally explain to another (a friend at work, a reflection in a mirror, or even a pillow named "Ed") what the Industrial Revolution was all about, what brought it on, and what the effects of it on the world have been. This verbal review helps students tie concepts together, know what they understand and what they don't, and prepare for tests.

Elaborative verbal rehearsals are another checkpoint where distance learners pause to reflect on what was learned and understood. Working independently with an imaginary audience or with a real audience allows students to self-monitor, become aware of what they understand, and make the material meaningful through personal examples.

5. References:

Dembo, M. (2004). *Motivation and learning strategies for college success* (2nd ed.). Mahwah, NJ: Erlbaum.

Pressley, M., Wood, E., Woloshyn, V., Martin, V., King, A., & Menke, D. (1992). Encouraging mindful use of prior knowledge: Attempting to construct explanatory answers facilitates learning. *Educational Psychologist, 27,* 91–109.

Simpson, M., & Nist, S. (2000). An update on strategic learning: It's more than textbook reading strategies. *Journal of Adolescent and Adult Literacy, 43,* 528–542.

Simpson, M., Olejnik, S., Tam, A., & Supattathum, S. (1994). Elaborative verbal rehearsals and college students' cognitive performance. *Journal of Educational Psychology, 86,* 267–278.

6. Glossary: **Elaboration:** Integrating meaningful knowledge into long-term memory through adding detail, summarizing, and creating examples and analogies (Dembo, 2004).

Meaningful learning: A process of learning whereby a student attempts to make sense of the material so it will be stored in long-term memory and retrieved when needed (Dembo, 2004).

Rehearsal: The process of repeating information, synthesized with personal experiences and examples, verbally to another person or to an imaginary audience (Simpson, Olejnik, Tam, & Supattathum, 1994).

Rote learning: A process of learning whereby students learn through repetition without trying to make any sense of the material (Dembo, 2004).

7. User: Instructional designer

STRATEGIES BASED ON GENERATION OF HIGHER LEVEL QUESTIONS

1. Guideline: When thought-provoking questions about learned material are generated by students, deeper understanding and higher academic performance results.

2. Guideline based on: Research

3. Degree of confidence: High

4. Comments: Higher level questions are thought-provoking questions that require synthesis, elaboration, application, and prediction of ideas (i.e., What are the strengths and weaknesses of . . . ? How does . . . affect . . . ? Why is . . . important? Compare . . . and . . . with regard to . . . . etc.; see King, 1992). These questions can be formed before, during, and/or after reading. Before reading, predictions can be made; during reading, inferences and examples emerge; and after reading, synthesis and application of ideas are possible. Prior knowledge is engaged to explain and connect concepts, and learning is deposited into long-term memory. Using a variety of such question stems encourages students to think about a given concept in different ways, and when this process is used by pairs or groups of students, different perspectives must be addressed. Similarly, group questioning provides opportunities for individuals to think about what they understood and be confronted by what they might not have understood. Research shows that groups and individuals that use higher level question stems show greater achievement on academic measures (King, 1992). Some training in generating higher level questions may be necessary in order for students to benefit fully from their use.

This activity is a particularly effective learning strategy for distance learners. They can use higher level questions whether interacting with written text, Internet peer chats, or virtual lectures. Higher level questions can be used to self-test as a test preparation strategy with the goal of predicting actual test questions.

5. References:

Dembo, M. (2004). *Motivation and learning strategies for college success* (2nd ed.). Mahwah, NJ: Erlbaum.

King, A. (1990). Enhancing peer interaction and learning in the classroom through reciprocal questioning. *American Educational Research Journal, 27,* 664–687.

King, A. (1992). Facilitating elaborative learning through guided student-generated questioning. *Educational Psychologist, 27,* 111–126.

Simpson, M., & Nist, S. (2000). An update on strategic learning: It's more than textbook reading strategies. *Journal of Adolescent and Adult Literacy, 43,* 528–542.

6. Glossary:

Elaboration: Integrating meaningful knowledge into long-term memory through adding detail, summarizing, creating examples, and making analogies (Dembo, 2004).

Higher level questions: Thought-provoking questions that require synthesis, elaboration, application, and prediction of ideas (King, 1992).
Long-term memory: Memory over extended periods of time, ranging from hours to days and years. Long-term memory is the permanent repository for acquired information.

7. User: Instructional designer

STRATEGIES BASED ON OUTLINE-FORMATTED NOTES

1. Guideline: Students who take and review outline-style notes comprehend more than students who do not.

2. Guideline based on: Research

3. Degree of confidence: Medium

4. Comments: The number of ideas included in notes is positively related to test performance. In other words, the more extensive notes students have, the better their chances are of performing well on academic measures. Research has been conducted showing that the process of taking notes aids later recall of material, and that reviewing notes is correlated with higher test scores (Kiewra, Benton, Kim, Risch, & Christensen, 1995). The outline format of notes is generally seen as an effective way of aiding both the process of note-taking (getting down all the key ideas) and the product of note-taking (test review and performance). Students that are left to note-take without specific guidance are reported to gather only 30% of the key ideas (Kiewra et al., 1995). This percentage significantly increases when the outline format is used. The internal connections between ideas become more apparent when notes are taken in outline format. This understanding of the relationship between concepts prepares students to relate the material to prior knowledge and elaborate on it mentally, reaching deeper understanding. It is important to mention that the cited research was conducted in a lecture-based setting. However, there is reason to believe that findings transfer to the text-based setting.

Since students in distance learning settings generally do not have the opportunity to both read the material and hear it in a lecture, the quality of their notes taken during reading is an important factor in retention of material.

5. References:

Dembo, M. (2004). *Motivation and learning strategies for college success* (2nd ed.). Mahwah, NJ: Erlbaum.

Kiewra, K. (1989). A review of note-taking: The encoding–storage paradigm and beyond. *Educational Psychology Review, 1,* 147–172.

Kiewra, K., & Benton, S. (1988). The relationship between information-processing ability and notetaking. *Contemporary Educational Psychology, 13,* 33–44.

Kiewra, K., Benton, S., Kim, S., Risch, N., & Christensen, M. (1995). Effects of note-taking format and study technique on recall and relational performance. *Contemporary Educational Psychology, 20,* 172–187.

Simpson, M., & Nist, S. (2000). An update on strategic learning: It's more than textbook reading strategies. *Journal of Adolescent and Adult Literacy, 43,* 528–542.

6. Glossary:

Elaboration: Integrating meaningful knowledge into long-term memory through adding detail, summarizing, and creating examples and analogies (Dembo, 2004).

Outline: Information grouped into subordinate relationship in notes, with topic headings extending farther to the left while subordinate ideas are included under the superordinate ideas and indented to the right (Kiewra et al., 1995).

7. User:

Instructional designer

STRATEGIES BASED ON TEST PREPARATION

1. Guideline: Students who adjust their study strategies to match testing demands have higher test scores than students who do not.

2. Guideline based on: Research

3. Degree of confidence: High

4. Comments: Students who adjust their test-taking strategies according to the demands of the test have higher test scores (Pressley, Yokoi, van Meter, Van Etten, & Freebern, 1997). The requirements of a history test may be different from the requirements of a math test. The history test may focus on memory for names and dates, whereas the math test may require application of concepts. Similarly, the test in one professor's history class may require different things than the test of a different history professor. Memory-focused tests have different cognitive demands than do application-type tests. Therefore, different study strategies will need to be employed. Morris, Bransford, and Franks (1977) called the ability of students to choose appropriate strategies for the individual test "transfer appropriate processing." They noted that students often do not appropriately adjust their strategies. Students should know what the format of the test will be, and use any available practice tests to guide them in their study strategy selection. When memory is the focus, repeatedly going over the material would be appropriate. However, when application or analyses are called for, more elaborative strategies will be required to be adequately prepared.

In the distance learning setting, students work more independently. They do not have peer interaction that might aid them in selecting appropriate test preparation study strategies. It is especially important for distance learners to be self-regulated students who are metacognitively aware, possess various study skills, and are prepared to select the study strategy that best corresponds to the test demands.

5. *References:*

Dembo, M. (2004). *Motivation and learning strategies for college success* (2nd ed.). Mahwah, NJ: Erlbaum.

Fleming, V. M. (2002). Improving students' exam performance by introducing study strategies and goal setting. *Teaching of Psychology, 29,* 115–119.

Kitsantas, A. (2002). Test preparation and performance: A self-regulatory analysis. *Journal of Experimental Education, 70,* 101–113.

Morris, L. W., Bransford, J. D., & Franks, J. J. (1977). Levels of processing versus transfer appropriate processing. *Journal of Verbal Learning and Verbal Behavior, 16,* 519–533.

Pressley, M., Yokoi, L., van Meter, P., Van Etten, S., & Freebern, G. (1997). Some of the reasons preparing for exams is so hard: What can be done to make it easier? *Educational Psychology Review, 9,* 1–38.

6. *Glossary:*

Cognition: The role of the learner's mental processing of information (Dembo, 2004).

Learning strategies: The techniques or methods students use to acquire information (Dembo, 2004).

Metacognition: The knowledge of one's own thinking processes and ability to regulate these processes (Dembo, 2004).

Self-regulated learning: Learning that occurs primarily from the influence of students' self-generated thoughts, feelings, strategies, and behaviors that are oriented toward the attainment of goals (Dembo, 2004).

7. *User:*

Instructional designer

STRATEGIES BASED ON HELP SEEKING

1. Guideline: Learners who are motivated to achieve tend to seek help from social (i.e., teachers or classmates) and/or nonsocial sources (i.e., written sources) when faced with complex and/or difficult tasks.

2. Guideline based on: Research

3. Degree of confidence: Medium

4. Comments: One of the distinguishing characteristics of self-regulated learners is their ability to seek academic assistance in an adaptive manner to optimize learning. *Adaptive help seeking* is used by self-regulatory learners to confront difficulties by persisting until they recognize additional effort would be unproductive and then seeking help in ways that not only allow them to succeed but help them become more autonomous learners (Karabenick & Knapp, 1991). However, research suggests that the students who need help the most are generally the least likely to ask for it (Newman, 1994).

The importance of the social context in distance learning has been widely discussed (Hara & Kling, 2000; Major & Levenberg, 1999). The social context of learning refers to both collaboration with and feedback from online classmates and instructors, as well as the learner's ability to identify nonsocial resources (e.g., supplementary instructional materials). Distance learners must be able to determine where and how to seek help, and make decisions concerning the most appropriate sources for such help.

5. References: Hara, N., & Kling, R. (2000). *Students' distress with a Web-based distance education course* (CSI Working Paper). Bloomington: Indiana University, Center for Social Informatics. Retrieved December 26, 2003, from http://www.slis.indiana.edu/CSI/wp00-01.htm

Karabenick, S. A., & Knapp, J. R. (1991). Relationship of academic help seeking to the use of learning strategies and other instrumental achievement behavior in college students. *Journal of Educational Psychology, 83,* 221–230.

Major, H., & Levenberg, N. (1999, January). Learner success in distance education environments: A shared responsibility. *The Technology Source* [Online]. Retrieved March 3, 2004, from http://ts.mivu.org/default.asp ?show=article&id=71&action=print

Newman, R. S. (1994). Adaptive help seeking: A strategy of self-regulated learning. In D. Schunk & B. Zimmerman (Eds.), *Self-regulation of learning and performance: Issues and educational applications* (pp. 283–301). Hillsdale, NJ: Erlbaum.

Ryan, A., Pintrich, P., & Midgley, C. (2001). Avoiding seeking help in the classroom: Who and why? *Educational Psychology Review, 13,* 93–114.

Zimmerman, B. J. (1998). Academic studying and the development of personal skill: A self-regulatory perspective. *Educational Psychologist, 33,* 73–86.

6. Glossary:

Adaptive help seeking: Used by self-regulatory learners to confront difficulties by persisting until they recognize that additional effort would be unproductive, and seek help in ways that not only allow them to succeed but help them become more autonomous learners (Karabenick & Knapp, 1991).

Self-regulatory process of help seeking: The process of choosing specific models, teachers, or books to assist in learning (Zimmerman, 1998).

7. User:

Instructional designer

STRATEGIES BASED ON TIME MANAGEMENT

1. Guideline:

Students who use their time efficiently are more likely to learn more successfully than students who do not have good time management skills.

2. Guideline based on: Research

3. Degree of confidence: Medium

4. Comments:

Successful students know how to manage their time in order to learn and accomplish necessary tasks. Self-regulated students know how to manage their time because they are aware of deadlines, how long it will take to complete each assignment, and their own learning processes. The greater such awareness is, the better the time management skills will be, meaning that more material will be read, reviewed, and elaborated upon (Zimmerman & Greenberg, 1994). In this way, time management improves achievement. Britton and Tesser (1991) suggested that time management measures are more predictive of academic achievement level than is the SAT score. One reason that self-regulated students with good time management skills may achieve so much academically could be because they tend to spend more time on difficult items than easier ones (Le Ny, Denhiere, & Le Taillanter, 1972). Time management skills can be learned, and subsequent efforts by students to manage their study time do make a difference academically. As time management skills are refined, more time is spent on task, procrastination decreases, tasks are completed on time, and chances of academic achievement and success improve. Additionally, as use of time improves, individuals show increased intrinsic interest and enhanced personal perceptions (Hall & Hursch, 1981–82).

In a distance learning setting, goal setting, planning, and time management are often the sole responsibility of the student, who has little or no interaction with other students or the instructor. In order to successfully complete all assignments and acquire the necessary information, students in such settings will need to be able to pace themselves, using time management skills to distribute learning and complete assigned work over time.

5. References:

Britton, B. K., & Tesser, A. (1991). Effects of time management practices on college grades. *Journal of Educational Psychology, 83,* 405–410.

Hall, B. L., & Hursch, D. E. (1981-82). An evaluation of the effects of a time management training program on work efficiency. *Journal of Organizational Behavior Management, 3*(4), 73–96.

Le Ny, J. F., Denhiere, G., & Le Taillanter, D. (1972). Regulation of study-time and interstimulus similarity in self-paced learning conditions. *Acta Psychologica, 36,* 280–289.

Zimmerman, B. J. (1998). Academic studying and the development of personal skill: A self-regulatory perspective. *Educational Psychologist, 33*(2/3), 73–86.

Zimmerman, B. J., & Greenberg, D. (1994). Self-regulating academic study time: A strategy approach. In D. H. Schunk & B. J. Zimmerman (Eds.), *Self-regulation of learning and performance: Issues and educational applications* (pp. 181–199). Hillsdale, NJ: Erlbaum.

6. Glossary:

Time management: The ability to accurately assess the time required to complete a given task, plan accordingly to appropriate the needed time, and successfully complete the task (Zimmerman & Greenberg, 1994).

7. User:

Instructional designer

STRATEGIES BASED ON GOAL SETTING

1. Guideline: Students with specific, challenging goals outper-
                              form students with general, easy, or no goals.

2. Guideline based on: Research

3. Degree of confidence: High

4. Comments: There are many academic benefits to goal set
                              ting. Goals direct attention, mobilize effort,
                              increase persistence, and motivate strategy
                              development. As students select and pursue
                              goals, they are able to progress personally, gain
                              feedback, and self-monitor their progress. They
                              become more self-motivated. Students with spe-
                              cific, challenging goals outperform those with
                              general, easy, or no goals. Effective goals are
                              short term (current) and so ask learners to
                              accomplish specific tasks today or, at the most,
                              this week (longer-term goals do not necessarily
                              help performance). It is important that students
                              have the ability to attain or at least approach the
                              specific, challenging goal; for academic benefits
                              to accrue, the goal cannot be out of reach and
                              unrealistic (Locke & Latham, 2002).

                              In a distance learning setting, self-selected
                              goals can give the student a sense of control, as
                              well as structure. There is little or no interaction
                              with an instructor, and the pace at which mate-
                              rial is covered will depend almost entirely on the
                              individual student. In order to set and maintain
                              an appropriate pace, goal setting and self-moni-
                              toring must occur. The material to be covered
                              must be broken down into monthly and weekly
                              goals. Daily tasks and schedules need to be set
                              up, adhered to, evaluated, reevaluated, and
                              adjusted as necessary.

                              Except for highly novel and complex tasks
                              (Kanfer, Ackerman, Murta, Dugdale, & Nelson,
                              1994), "Three C" goals (concrete, current, and
                              challenging) seem to help both learning and
                              motivation. On the motivation side, Locke and
                              Latham (2002) suggested that specific Three C

goals facilitate active choice by encouraging "relevant" activities for goal achievement; they encourage appropriate mental effort, since adults need to adjust their effort to the level of the goal, and people tend to persist in the face of distractions until they attain their goals.

5. References: Curry, J., Haderlie, S., Ku, T., Lawless, K., Lemon, M., & Wood, R. (1999). Specified learning goals and their effect on learners' representations of a hypertext reading environment. *International Journal of Instructional Media, 26,* 43–51.

Dembo, M. (2004). *Motivation and learning strategies for college success* (2nd ed.). Mahwah, NJ: Erlbaum.

Kanfer, R., Ackerman, P. L., Murta, P. C., Dugdale, P., & Nelson, L. (1994). Goal setting, conditions of practice and task performance: A resource allocation perspective. *Journal of Applied Psychology, 79,* 826–835.

Locke, E. A., & Latham, G. P. (2002). Building a practically useful theory of goal setting and task motivation. *American Psychologist, 57,* 705–717.

6. Glossary: **Attention:** A selective process that controls awareness of events in the environment (Dembo, 2004).

Goal setting: The process of setting a course to attain a specific desired end by articulating subtasks and setting timelines for completion (Locke & Latham, 2002).

7. User: Instructional designer

STRATEGIES BASED ON TEST ANXIETY REDUCTION

1. Guideline: Students' test anxiety can be reduced and, often, test performance increased by using a variety of educational interventions.

2. Guideline based on: Research

3. Degree of confidence: Medium

4. Comments:

Test anxiety is a specific form of anxiety about academic and ability evaluations that can negatively influence students' motivation and academic performance. Test anxiety is a common problem, particularly among adult learners who are concerned about their ability to meet expectations and have a fear of failure. Anxiety can impact students at two major stages: studying and test taking. While studying, some students think about lack of ability, poor expectations, and the futility and ineffectiveness of their study. Anxiety interferes with appropriate organization of the content materials at this point. Students threatened by failure may also become involved in avoidance behaviors, such as irrational goal setting or procrastination, that will further erode their study effectiveness. In the test-taking stage, students attempt to retrieve what they have learned, sometimes in the face of great physical tension and worry. Anxiety at this stage interferes with the retrieval of information.

The most effective educational interventions used to treat test anxiety include cognitive-behavioral treatments such as relaxation techniques, provision of appropriate modeling of positive and negative self-talk, and practice of such skills in a testing environment (Hembree, 1988). It is important to analyze in which of the stages anxiety is occurring. Does the student have poor study skills? If so, some skill training in learning strategies will be required. If the student has good study skills, then a cognitive modification program aimed at reducing anxiety at test time would be effective.

5. References:

Awang-Hashim, R., O'Neil, H. F., & Hocevar, D. (2002). Ethnicity, effort, self-efficacy, worry, and statistics in Malaysia: A construct validation of the state-trait motivation model. *Educational Assessment, 8,* 341–364.

Hembree, R. (1988). Correlates, causes, effects, and treatment of test anxiety. *Review of Educational Research, 58,* 47–77.

Liebert, R., & Morris, L. (1967). Cognitive and emotional components of test anxiety: A distinction and some initial data. *Psychological Report, 20,* 975–978.

Zeidner, M. (1998). Coping with test situations: Resources, strategies, and adaptational outcomes. In *Test anxiety: The state of the art* (pp. 305–331). New York: Plenum Press.

6. Glossary:

Relaxation training: Involves a variety of interventions that include methods of breath control training and muscle relaxation (Hembree, 1988).

Test anxiety: Debilitating personal outcomes when a person is required to take some assessment of his or her competency. It consists of two components: worry and emotionality. Worry is the cognitive expression of concern about one's own performance, and emotionality refers to physiological reactions to the test situation (Liebert & Morris, 1967).

7. User:

Instructional designer

CHAPTER 5

ASSESSMENT STRATEGIES

**Eva L. Baker, Zenaida Aguirre-Muñoz, Jia Wang,
and David Niemi**
*University of California, Los Angeles/National Center
for Research on Evaluation, Standards,
and Student Testing (CRESST)*

The following guidelines are presented in this chapter:

Strategies Based on Validity
Strategies Based on Cognitive Demands
Strategies Based on Domain Representation
Strategies Based on Test Specifications
Strategies Based on Scoring
Strategies Based on Reliability
Strategies Based on Reporting
Strategies Based on Formative Assessment
Strategies Based on Certification Tests: Cut Scores
Strategies Based on Formative Evaluation
Strategies Based on Summative Evaluation

What Works in Distance Learning: Guidlines, pages 65–88
Copyright © 2005 by Information Age Publishing
All rights of reproduction in any form reserved.

STRATEGIES BASED ON VALIDITY

1. Guideline: Validity is the degree to which appropriate inferences, conclusions, or decisions can be made
from test results and depends fundamentally on
the purpose for which the test is being used.

2. Guideline based on: Theory and research

3. Degree of confidence: High

4. Comments: Validity refers to the degree to which empirical
evidence and theory support the adequacy and
appropriateness of interpretations and subsequent actions, based on test scores (Messick,
1995a). Validity is established by describing the
purpose of the test and then creating a logical
and/or empirically based argument that supports the use of the findings for the intended
purposes. The procedure for validation involves
finding evidence that will support or disconfirm
the interpretations to be made from test scores.
Over time, available validity evidence is augmented by new empirical findings, perhaps
involving similar settings or examinees. The
closer the match of the situation, examinees,
and purposes, the more likely the empirical
information will be useful, because validity is
specific to the examinee group, context, and
purpose of the assessment. It can only be investi-
gated when examination conditions are known
and standardized.

Although validity had been divided into sub-
types (i.e., content, predictive, criterion, or construct), newer thinking emphasizes that validity
is a unified idea related to the appropriateness
of the interpretation and may use a wide range
of evidence to form the conclusion. Validity
depends on how the test is used rather than
details of the test properties.

Four essential elements are required for a test
to be valid. First, the test items must be within
the boundaries of the domain to be assessed
(Messick, 1995b). Second, the items must fully

represent the domain being assessed (Messick, 1995a, 1995b). This ensures that the data gathered accurately reflect the important components of the domain being assessed. Items might be selected in terms of what characterizes and differentiates expertise in a particular area. Third, the items must not give credit to performance that is not relevant to the domain being tested (Haertel & Linn, 1996). Last, validity implies fairness to identifiable subgroups of examinees. Fairness issues to consider are fair access to the test and fair administration, opportunity to learn the tested domain, equitable treatment for all examinees, and bias related to examinees' background factors.

5. References:

American Educational Research Association, American Psychological Association, & National Council on Measurement in Education. (1999). *Standards for educational and psychological testing.* Washington, DC: American Educational Research Association.

Haertel, E., & Linn, R. L. (1996). Comparability. In G. W. Phillips (Ed.), *Technical issues in large-scale performance assessment* (NCES Rep. No. 96-802, pp. 59–78). Washington, DC: U.S. Department of Education, Office of Educational Research and Improvement, National Center for Education Statistics.

Messick, S. (1989). Validity. In R. L. Linn (Ed.), *Educational measurement* (3rd ed., pp. 13–103). New York: Macmillan.

Messick, S. (1995a). Standards of validity and the validity of standards in performance assessment. *Educational Measurement: Issues and Practice, 14*(4), 5–8.

Messick, S. (1995b). Validity of psychological assessment: Validation of inferences from persons' responses and performances as scientific inquiry into score meaning. *American Psychologist, 50,* 741–749.

6. Glossary:

Construct validity: "Is evaluated by investigating what qualities a test measures, that is, by determining the degree to which certain explanatory concepts or constructs account for performance on the test" (Messick, 1989, p. 16).

Content validity: "Is evaluated by showing how well the content of the test samples the class of situations or subject matter about which conclusions are to be drawn" (Messick, 1989, p. 16).

Criterion-related validity: "Is evaluated by comparing the test scores with one or more external variables (called criteria) considered to provide a direct measure of the characteristics or behavior in question" (Messick, 1989, p. 16).

Predictive validity: "Indicates the extent to which an individual's future level on the criterion is predicted from prior test performance" (Messick, 1989, p. 16).

7. Users: Program manager, assessment designer

STRATEGIES BASED ON COGNITIVE DEMANDS

1. Guideline: To ensure that assessments reflect the types of learning to be assessed, assessment design and validation should be preceded by a cognitive analysis (cognitive demands) of the task/performance, divided into aspects that are domain independent and those specially addressed to the domain of learning and assessment.

2. Guideline based on: Research and expert opinion

3. Degree of confidence: High

4. Comments: Assessment specifications should explicitly reference both the models of cognitive demand in the task (e.g., content understanding or problem solving) and the cognitive requirements of desired performance in the specific content area. Assessment development should have a scientific basis; for example, specification of the domain to be assessed should draw on cognitive research in the domain, and task design should be informed by cognitive analysis and empirical testing of tasks.

Model-based assessment design is an approach to the development and validation of assessments based on the cognitive demands of the task nested within a particular content area, and the application of domain-independent specifications that serve as templates for the creation of assessments comparable across different topic or content areas. Performances can be analyzed initially in terms of five families of domain-independent cognitive demands (Baker, 1997): content understanding, problem solving, metacognition, communication, and teamwork.

5. References:

American Educational Research Association, American Psychological Association, & National Council on Measurement in Education. (1999). *Standards for educational and psychological testing.* Washington, DC: American Educational Research Association.

Baker, E. L. (1997). Model-based performance assessment. *Theory Into Practice, 36,* 247–254.

Baker, E. L., & Mayer, R. E. (1999). Computer-based assessment of problem solving. *Computers in Human Behavior, 15,* 269–282.

Hsieh, I.-L., & O'Neil, H. F., Jr. (2002). Types of feedback in a computer-based collaborative problem-solving group task. *Computers in Human Behavior, 18,* 699–715.

Mayer, R. E., & Wittrock, M. C. (1996). Problem-solving transfer. In D. C. Berliner & R. C. Calfee (Eds.), *Handbook of educational psychology* (pp. 47–62). New York: Simon & Schuster Macmillan.

Niemi, D. (1997). Cognitive science, expert-novice research, and performance assessment. *Theory Into Practice, 36,* 239–246.

6. Glossary:

Cognitive demands: To analyze the "cognitive demands" of a performance means to specify the knowledge and mental skills required to complete that performance successfully (Baker & Mayer, 1999).

Communication: Representation of information to another person (Baker, 1997). Modes of communication include speech, gesture, text, and graphical representations (e.g., pictures, diagrams, graphs).

Content knowledge: Knowledge in a specific subject area, including (a) core principles and concepts, (b) factual knowledge, (c) procedures for solving problems in the subject area, (d) knowledge about when and how to use subject area knowledge, and (e) knowledge about how new information in the subject area is developed, justified, and evaluated (Niemi, 1997).

Metacognition: Planning and monitoring one's progress toward solving a problem (Hsieh & O'Neil, 2002).

Problem solving: Cognitive processing "directed at achieving a goal when no solution method is obvious to the problem solver" (Mayer & Wittrock, 1996, p. 47).

Teamwork: Refers to work on tasks in which members of the group must interact with each other in order to accomplish the task (Hsieh & O'Neil, 2002).

7. Users: Program manager, assessment designer

STRATEGIES BASED ON DOMAIN REPRESENTATION

1. Guideline: Validity investigations should examine and describe the degree to which content on tests is relevant to and representative of the domain assessed, particularly to avoid construct under-representation.

2. Guideline based on: Research and expert opinion

3. Degree of confidence: High

4. Comments: Tests must contain adequate sampling of items or tasks that are representative of the content domain to be assessed. Content representation can be best determined by experts in the content domain who match test specifications and test item features. Their task is to identify gaps, under- and overrepresentation, and content errors, and to ensure that the administration of the test itself provides adequate stimuli. Individual items should be judged for their relevance to the content domain and the collection of items evaluated for representativeness of the domain of competency to be tested. The test should capture all important parts of the domain, content as well as processes (i.e., what people actually do in the performance domain), including characteristics that distinguish expert knowledge and skill.

Review of scoring criteria should be part of this process for open-ended tasks, augmented by the presentation of exemplars of work at different proficiency levels. Degree of agreement among raters should be reported. A related concern is the inclusion of items or tasks that are too broad and that inadvertently assess knowledge or skills not outlined in the test specifications. Such items would introduce construct-irrelevant variance— another major threat to validity.

5. References:

American Educational Research Association, American Psychological Association, & National Council on Measurement in Education. (1999). *Standards for educational and psychological testing.* Washington, DC: American Educational Research Association.

Linn, R. L., Baker, E. L., & Dunbar, S. B. (1991). Complex, performance assessment: Expectations and validation criteria. *Educational Researcher, 20*(8), 15–21.

Messick, S. (1996). Validity of performance assessment. In G. Phillips (Ed.), *Technical issues in large-scale performance assessment* (pp. 1–18). Washington, DC: U.S. Department of Education, National Center for Education Statistics.

6. Glossary: **Construct-irrelevant variance:** Occurs when an assessment task includes skills not included in the domain, requiring abilities for successful completion of the test that are not explicit goals of instruction. An example of construct-irrelevant variance is difficult language used in test items or a task that incorporates complex linguistic structures when its intent is to measure knowledge of a particular content area (e.g., mathematics; Messick, 1996).

Construct underrepresentation: Occurs when an assessment is too narrow, missing important facets of the overall content domain and the constructs of which the domain is comprised (Messick, 1996).

7. User: Assessment designer

STRATEGIES BASED ON TEST SPECIFICATIONS

1. Guideline: Prior to item, test, or task development, test specifications should be prepared to guide the test designers' attention to key elements of the test such as test purposes, intellectual skills, content, and format of the test.

2. Guideline based on: Research and expert opinion

3. Degree of confidence: High

4. Comments: Test specifications refer to the test framework containing information about the format of items, tasks, or questions; the response format or conditions for responding; the type of scoring procedures; the intended use of results; the boundaries of content knowledge; cognitive demands of performance and situations on the test; sample items and scoring procedures; the composition of the entire test; test administration procedures; and the intended population of test takers. Test specifications may also include information regarding the desired psychometric properties of the items, such as difficulty and discrimination, as well as the desired test properties, such as test difficulty and reliability. All subsequent test development activities are guided by the test specifications.

The first step in generating test specifications is to have clearly in mind the respondents and the purpose or purposes for which the results will be used. The three common purposes are to support instruction, to provide individual or team certification, and to provide data for use in program evaluation. Test specifications need to be reviewed for clarity and compared to the intended goals of the training system, and to any specific goals for transferring or applying knowledge to new domains or situations. Also, test specifications need to be reviewed to ensure that the test fully represents the range of knowledge required.

The major usefulness of specifications comes in the review of the match among individual items, curriculum, and test specifications. This review requires that a judgment be made of the balance among content areas, avoiding construct underrepresentation. However, overrepresentation may be needed for important or especially difficult tasks. In addition to providing evidence that the individual items and the test as a whole are measuring the targeted cognitive and content domains, specifications may yield sufficient items to provide stable measures of subskills or objectives. Specifications should demand detailed information about the intended examinee group and sample test items, scoring schemes that include expected performance levels, and reporting plans.

5. References: American Educational Research Association, American Psychological Association, & National Council on Measurement in Education. (1999). *Standards for educational and psychological testing.* Washington, DC: American Educational Research Association.

Baker, E. L., Freeman, M., & Clayton, S. (1991). Cognitive assessment of history for large-scale testing. In M. C. Wittrock & E. L. Baker (Eds.), *Testing and cognition* (pp. 131–153). Englewood Cliffs, NJ: Prentice-Hall.

Messick, S. (1995). Standards of validity and the validity of standards in performance assessment. *Educational Measurement: Issues and Practice, 14*(4), 5–8.

6. Glossary: **Construct underrepresentation:** Occurs when an assessment is too narrow, missing important facets of the overall content domain and the constructs of which the domain is comprised (Messick, 1995).

Content domain: Refers to the process of delineating the boundaries of the construct(s) to be assessed and expressed through current models of learning and instruction. This process involves identifying and clarifying the specific knowledge, skills, related mental processes, and additional attributes and/or attitudes that should be assessed (Baker, Freeman, & Clayton, 1991).

7. User: Assessment designer

STRATEGIES BASED ON SCORING

1. Guideline: A scoring framework should include information on the measurement scale, scoring criteria, performance descriptions of each criterion at each point on the scale, and sample responses that illustrate the various levels of performance.

2. Guideline based on: Theory and research

3. Degree of confidence: High

4. Comments: Different scoring frameworks should be followed for choice–response assessment and performance-based assessment. With choice–response assessment (e.g., multiple-choice, true or false, or matching test items), the scoring procedure consists of (a) specifying the answer key for each item, (b) a rule for adding up the scores, and (c) the actual scoring of the assessment. The scoring, typically done by machines, is fast, economical, and relatively free of scoring error. The one major disadvantage is that choice–response assessment is susceptible to guessing and decontextualizes knowledge assessment.

Performance-based assessment (e.g., essay items or simulations) requires examinees to construct their own responses to questions or prompts. The assessment imitates or creates the real context in which the examinees can demonstrate their knowledge and skills. Performance-based assessment requires human judgment. The scoring is usually done by raters and requires careful selection of raters and detailed design and administration of training and scoring sessions. The typical scoring process includes the preparation of a scoring rubric for each task, the preparation of training and qualifying packets consisting of actual responses, rater training and calibrating, scoring, and monitoring of raters' work. Assignment of work to be rated should be at random to avoid rater bias. Alternative techniques for scoring performance-based assessments are holistic scoring and analytic scoring. Because it includes scores for multiple dimensions, analytic scoring is usually preferred for providing useful information to improve instruction. Holistic scoring is preferred when an overall evaluation is needed.

5. References:

American Educational Research Association, American Psychological Association, & National Council on Measurement in Education. (1999). *Standards for educational and psychological testing.* Washington, DC: American Educational Research Association.

Arter, J., & McTighe, J. (2001). *Scoring rubrics in the classroom: Using performance criteria for assessing and improving student performance.* Thousand Oaks, CA: Corwin Press.

Haladyna, T. M., Downing, S. M., & Rodriguez, M. C. (2002). A review of multiple-choice item-writing guidelines for classroom assessment. *Applied Measurement in Education, 15,* 309–334.

Messick, S. (1989). Validity. In R. L. Linn (Ed.), *Educational measurement* (3rd ed., pp. 13–103). New York: American Council on Education/Macmillan.

6. Glossary: **Analytic scoring:** Evaluates examinee's work across multiple dimensions of performance. Individual scores for each dimension are reported (Arter & McTighe, 2001).

Holistic scoring: Evaluates examinee's work based on the overall quality of the work. Only a single score is reported (Arter & McTighe, 2001).

Score: A score indicates a performance level. To understand a score, one needs information on the associated task and the performance of others (Messick, 1989).

7. Users: Program manager, assessment designer

STRATEGIES BASED ON RELIABILITY

1. Guideline: A reliable test should give accurate and similar scores from one occasion to another, from one form of a test to another, and from one rater to another.

2. Guideline based on: Theory and research

3. Degree of confidence: High

4. Comments: Traditionally, the reliability of a measure was defined as its consistency in giving the same results for the same person over time. More recently, reliability is thought to consist of both accuracy and consistency. There are two testing theories that provide reliability indices: classical true-score theory and generalizability (G) theory. The fundamental assumption of the classical true-score theory is that the score of an examinee consists of two parts: true score and error of measurement. There are mainly three methods associated with estimating a reliability coefficient: test–retest, parallel forms, and internal consistency. Cronbach's alpha coefficient is one of the most frequently used internal consistency measures.

Dependability of behavioral measurements is the focus of G theory. Dependability refers to the accuracy of generalizing a person's observed score on one test to his or her average score across all possible testing conditions. G theory goes beyond classical true-score theory by estimating multiple sources of error in a measurement simultaneously in a single analysis. For example, if we give two forms of a test, on two different occasions, scored by five raters, the error of measurement would come from all three sources (i.e., forms, occasions, and raters), their interactions, and from unknown residual sources.

G theory provides a G coefficient to indicate the dependability level of a score and allows a design aspect that suggests how many test forms, raters, and so on are needed in order to have dependable scores. Research has documented that it is easier to obtain high degrees of rater agreement (with proper training) and more difficult to find high relationships for performance across tasks.

5. References:

Allen, M. J., & Yen, W. M. (1979). *Introduction to measurement theory.* Monterey, CA: Brooks-Cole.

American Educational Research Association, American Psychological Association, & National Council on Measurement in Education. (1999). *Standards for educational and psychological testing.* Washington, DC: American Educational Research Association.

Brennan, R. L. (2000). Performance assessments from the perspective of generalizability theory. *Applied Psychological Measurement, 24,* 339–353.

Moss, P. (1994). Can there be validity without reliability? *Educational Researcher, 23*(2), 5–12.

Webb, N. M., Shavelson, R. J., Kim, K.-S., & Chen, Z. (1989). Reliability (generalizability) of job performance measurements: Navy Machinist Mates. *Military Psychology, 1,* 91–110.

6. Glossary:

Accuracy: Refers to the degree that the test scores are free from measurement error (Moss, 1994).

Consistency: Refers to the extent a measure yields identical results from independent but interchangeable observations (Moss, 1994).

Parallel forms reliability coefficient: The relationship between observed scores from different forms of a test in which the forms are parallel to each other in all aspects except specific test items (Webb, Shavelson, Kim, & Chen, 1989).

Test–retest reliability coefficient: The relationship between observed scores from one test occasion to another (Webb et al., 1989).

True score: The average score across multiple independent administrations of the same test, which minimizes the measurement error (Allen & Yen, 1979).

7. Users:

Program manager, assessment designer

STRATEGIES BASED ON REPORTING

1. Guideline:

Reporting of test results should include information on test purpose(s), test content, the scoring scheme, reporting scale, test validity, and test accuracy, conveyed in nontechnical language.

2. Guideline based on:

Research and expert opinion

3. Degree of confidence:

Medium

4. Comments:

Reporting should include comparisons such as performance in relation to particular goals, standards, or overall competency areas. Results related to training are usually reported in terms of level of achievement attained (criterion referenced), but may be reported in terms of relative standing among a cohort or against an existing normative group (norm referenced), or in terms of individual or group progress. To judge the utility of the findings or standards, it is essential to report the magnitude of the measurement error and the level of accuracy given the examinee sample. Providing validity evidence on the link between a new assessment and existing measures increases the meaning and utility in terms of the test results.

Attention must be paid to the appropriateness of the form of reporting for different audiences or stakeholders. Appropriate levels of technical language, graphs, and acceptable documentation of technical data will vary for different audiences. Periodic studies of report comprehension for the report's principal users will increase the utility of report findings.

5. References: American Educational Research Association, American Psychological Association, & National Council on Measurement in Education. (1999). *Standards for educational and psychological testing.* Washington, DC: American Educational Research Association.

Burdette, P. (2001). Alternate assessment: Early highlights and pitfalls of reporting. *Assessment for Effective Intervention, 26*(2), 61–66.

Linn, R. L. (2000). Assessments and accountability. *Educational Researcher, 29*(2), 4–16.

6. Glossary: **Criterion-referenced test:** Provides a measure of the examinee's absolute performance level, whether meeting certain criteria or not (American Educational Research Association, American Psychological Association, & National Council on Measurement in Education, 1999).

Norm: A norm for a test indicates the current status of examinee performance. It is constructed from a representative sample of examinees who have taken the same test (American Educational Research Association, American Psychological Association, & National Council on Measurement in Education, 1999).

Norm-referenced test: Compares an examinee's performance to the norm. The test results indicate the relative position of the examinee to the norm (American Educational Research Association, American Psychological Association, & National Council on Measurement in Education, 1999).

Scale: In testing, a scale is a composite measure of several items with built-in logical or empirical structure (American Educational Research Association, American Psychological Association, & National Council on Measurement in Education, 1999).

7. Users: Program manager, assessment designer

STRATEGIES BASED ON FORMATIVE ASSESSMENT

1. Guideline: Tests given during instruction should provide information for feedback and motivation to the learner, guide the program to provide needed help, and give the instructional designer information about program strengths and weaknesses.

2. Guideline based on: Research and expert opinion

3. Degree of confidence: High

4. Comments: Obtaining information through embedded or explicit performance trials will give information about the degree to which a learner is achieving in specified skills, subskills, and content domains. The patterns of success and misunderstandings inferred from performance errors can guide immediate intervention or recommendations for help and be used to revise subsequent versions of the instruction.

Sometimes called "formative assessment" or diagnostic testing, testing to support instruction is intended to help students learn from errors or to provide elaboration as a consequence of performance during instruction (Black & Wiliam, 1998). One key point is that performance during instruction may follow different patterns that can predict desired outcomes. Obtaining such information is necessary but not sufficient to guarantee that performance will improve. Detailed feedback for the student may need to be supplemented by additional instructional experiences. Research supports the efficacy of providing detailed information for students about their responses, as well as advice on what they can do to improve. Students also benefit from training in self-assessment, which helps them understand the main goals of the instruction and determine what they need to do to master the content (Pellegrino, Chudowsky, & Glaser, 2001).

5. References:

Black, P., & Wiliam, D. (1998). Assessment and classroom learning. *Assessment in Education, 5,* 7–73.

Kluger, A. N., & DeNisi, A. (1996). The effects of feedback intervention on performance: A historical review, a meta-analysis, and a preliminary feedback intervention theory. *Psychological Bulletin, 119,* 254–284.

Pellegrino, J., Chudowsky, N., & Glaser, R. (Eds.). (2001). *Knowing what students know: The science and design of educational assessments* (Committee on the Foundations of Assessment, Board on Testing and Assessment, Center for Education, Division on Behavioral and Social Sciences and Education, National Research Council). Washington, DC: National Academy Press.

6. Glossary:

Formative testing or assessment: Involves systematic acquisition of student achievement or performance information, often obtained by posing a problem or asking direct questions about responses. It requires considerable interaction with the learner. Diagnostic data result in detailed feedback based on assessment results focused on the qualities of the student's current understanding, including systematic errors and misconceptions due to lack of prior knowledge or errors in strategy, levels of competence, and depth of knowledge (Black & Wiliam, 1998).

7. User: Assessment designer

STRATEGIES BASED ON CERTIFICATION TESTS: CUT SCORES

1. Guideline: The specification of the cut score of a certification test should be based on empirical studies that indicate accurate distinctions among levels of performance (i.e., acceptable and unacceptable).

2. Guideline based on: Research and expert opinion

3. Degree of confidence: High

4. Comments: Tests for certification are designed to determine whether the core knowledge and skills of a specified domain have been mastered by the candidate. Therefore, prior to test development, a clear statement of the objectives of the test should be prepared, in addition to a clear definition of the content domain to be covered in terms of the importance of the content for performance deemed to be adequate for certification. Two potential objectives are to identify those individuals successfully completing training and those best suited for an intended job classification. The level of performance required for passing a certification test should depend on the knowledge and skills necessary for acceptable performance in the job it is intended to predict.

Dividing examinees into various levels of success requires the identification of a passing or "cut" score. Arbitrary numerical specifications of cut scores, such as 70%, should be avoided because detailed information about the test, the job requirements, and their relationship is needed for setting adequate performance standards. A job or practice analysis provides the primary basis for defining the domain and the preliminary cut score and should be consistent with the objectives of the test and the level of feedback needed. This score cannot just be determined solely by expert judgment but needs to be empirically studied, using the tests with novices and with trained and expert performers. The validity of the inferences drawn from test performance depends on whether the cut score makes accurate distinctions between adequate and inadequate performance. If a test is not designed to provide information on how well an individual passed or how badly an individual failed, the test need only be precise around the vicinity of the cut score. However, when feedback is needed across the range of performance—about the degree of failure or success—precision throughout the score range is needed.

5. References: American Educational Research Association, American Psychological Association, & National Council on Measurement in Education. (1999). *Standards for educational and psychological testing.* Washington, DC: American Educational Research Association.

Haertel, E. H. (1999). Validity arguments for high-stakes testing: In search of the evidence. *Educational Measurement: Issues and Practice, 18*(4), 5–9.

Jaeger, R. M. (1998). Evaluating the psychometric qualities of the National Board for Professional Teaching Standards' Assessments: A methodological accounting. *Journal of Personnel Evaluation in Education, 12,* 189–210.

6. Glossary: **Cut score:** A specified point on a score scale, such that scores at or above that point are interpreted or acted upon differently from scores below that point (Jaeger, 1998).

7. User: Assessment designer

STRATEGIES BASED ON FORMATIVE EVALUATION

1. Guideline: Formative evaluation provides information that focuses on improvement of an innovation and is designed to assist the developer.

2. Guideline based on: Theory and research

3. Degree of confidence: High

4. Comments: Formative evaluation is a method that was created to assist in the development of instructional (training) programs. While the evaluation team maintains quasi-objectivity, they typically interact with and understand program goals, processes, and constraints at a deeper level than evaluation teams focused exclusively on bottom-line assessments of success or failure (i.e., outcomes-only, summative evaluation). Their intent is to assist their client (either funding agency or project staff) in using systematic data collection to promote the improvement of the effort.

Formative evaluation efforts are instituted at the outset of the development of an innovation and have a different purpose than summative evaluation. Formative evaluation addresses the effectiveness of the development procedures used, in order to predict whether the application of similar approaches is likely to have effective and efficient results. In that function, formative evaluation seeks to improve both the technology at large and the specific instances, addressed one at a time. The formative evaluation approach is designed so that its principal outputs are identification of the degree of success and failure of segments, components, and details of programs, rather than a simple, overall estimate of project success. This approach requires that data be developed to permit the isolation of elements for improvement and, ideally, the generation of remedial options to ensure that subsequent revisions have a higher probability of success.

Formative evaluation is strong in identifying what to do if the new system is not an immediate, unqualified success. Given that this state is most common in early stages of development, comparative, summative-type evaluations are usually mistimed and may create an unduly negative environment for productivity. Furthermore, because summative evaluation is typically not designed to pinpoint weaknesses and explore potential remedies, it provides almost no help in the development/improvement cycle that characterizes the systematic creation of new methods.

5. References:

Baker, E. L. (1974). Beyond objectives: Domain-referenced tests for evaluation and instructional improvement. In W. Hively (Ed.), *Domain-referenced testing* (pp. 16–30). Englewood Cliffs, NJ: Educational Technology Publications.

Baker, E. L. (1988). Evaluating new technology: Formative evaluation of intelligent computer-assisted instruction. In R. J. Seidel & P. D. Weddle (Eds.), *Computer-based instruction in military environments* (pp. 155–162). New York: Plenum Press.

Baker, E. L., & Herman, J. L. (2003). A distributed evaluation model. In G. Haertel & B. Means (Eds.), *Evaluating educational technology* (pp. 95–119). New York: Teachers College Press.

6. Glossary:

Formative evaluation: Begins and ends in the developmental stage of the program evaluation. It improves the program by providing information on implementation and progress (Baker, 1974).

Summative evaluation: Evaluation designed to present conclusions about the merit or worth of an object and recommendations about whether it should be retained, altered, or eliminated (see *Glossary of evaluation terms.* Kalamazoo: Western Michigan University, Evaluation Center. Retrieved July

26, 2002, from http://ec.wmich.edu/glos-sary). The final evaluation that determines whether the program has succeeded in reaching its goals and whether it should be implemented.

7. Users: Program manager, assessment designer

STRATEGIES BASED ON SUMMATIVE EVALUATION

1. Guideline: Summative evaluation should assist decision makers in their decisions on whether they should select, continue, modify, or drop a program.

2. Guideline based on: Theory and research

3. Degree of confidence: High

4. Comments: Test performance should be used in decisions judging the utility, appropriateness, implementation, and quality of the outcome of a program, usually in a comparative research design, contrasting performance of trainees under different training experiences, and evaluating them using common measures. Evaluate distance learning efforts using measures of implementation, outcomes, efficiencies, satisfaction, and long-term impact.

The issue of the effect of learning via distance using technology is still problematic, with one of the problems being that current research is not providing sufficiently robust data. A majority of articles on distance education are opinion pieces and how-to articles. Mixed results of actual research may be explained by the fact that the research is based on individual case studies, qualitative data, or self-report studies. Many studies in distance learning indicate that teaching and learning at a distance is as effective as traditional classroom instruction and results in high satisfaction when compared to traditional approaches. There is the call to incorporate evaluation models, such as Kirkpatrick's (1994) four-level approach.

After deciding on the purposes or goals of the evaluation, the decision makers should narrow the assessment search, defining the target population, the program participants, what should be evaluated, and the population to which the results are to be generalized. The cost and credibility of adopting an existing test meeting program purposes or goals should be compared with the cost of designing, administering, and reporting a new test. Summative evaluation can be supplemented with formative evaluation.

5. References:

American Educational Research Association, American Psychological Association, & National Council on Measurement in Education. (1999). *Standards for educational and psychological testing.* Washington, DC: American Educational Research Association.

Baker, E. L. (1974). Beyond objectives: Domain-referenced tests for evaluation and instructional improvement. In W. Hively (Ed.), *Domain-referenced testing* (pp. 16–30). Englewood Cliffs, NJ: Educational Technology Publications.

Berge, Z. L., & Mrozowski, S. (2001). Review of research in distance education, 1990–1999. *American Journal of Distance Education, 13*(3), 5–19.

Kirkpatrick, D. L. (1994). *Evaluating training programs: The four levels.* San Francisco: Berrett-Koehler.

6. Glossary:

Formative evaluation: Begins and ends in the developmental stage of the program evaluation. It improves the program by providing information on implementation and progress (Baker, 1974).

Kirkpatrick's four levels: A four-level model consisting of (1) reaction, (2) learning, (3) transfer, and (4) results. According to this model, evaluation should always begin with level one and then, as time and budget allow, should move sequentially through levels two, three, and four. [Hoffman, B. (Ed.).

(2004). *Encyclopedia of educational technology.* San Diego, CA: San Diego State University, Department of Educational Technology. Retrieved July 26, 2002, from http://ccoe.sdsu.edu/eet]

Summative evaluation: Evaluation designed to present conclusions about the merit or worth of an object and recommendations about whether it should be retained, altered, or eliminated (see *Glossary of evaluation terms.* Kalamazoo: Western Michigan University, Evaluation Center. Retrieved July 26, 2002, from http://ec.wmich.edu/glossary). The final evaluation that determines whether the program has succeeded in reaching its goals and whether it should be implemented.

7. Users: Program manager, assessment designer

CHAPTER 6

MOTIVATION STRATEGIES

Richard Clark
University of Southern California

The following guidelines are presented in this chapter:

Strategies Based on Increasing Student Motivation: Encouraging Active
Engagement and Persistence

Strategies Based on Increasing Student Motivation: Helping Learners
Invest Maximum Mental Effort

Strategies Based on Motivating Active Choice to Engage in Distance
Learning

Strategies Based on Motivating Persistence in the Face of Distractions

Strategies Based on Helping Learners Invest Maximum Mental Effort

Strategies Based on Increasing Learners' Self-Efficacy for Specific
Learning Tasks

Strategies Based on Decreasing Learner Procrastination

Strategies Based on Motivating Learners by Increasing the Value of
Learning Goals and Objectives

Strategies Based on the Motivational Impact of Effective Instructional
Models

Strategies Based on the Motivational Impact of Effective Performance
Attributions

What Works in Distance Learning: Guidlines, pages 89–109
Copyright © 2005 by Information Age Publishing
All rights of reproduction in any form reserved.

STRATEGIES BASED ON INCREASING STUDENT MOTIVATION: ENCOURAGING ACTIVE ENGAGEMENT AND PERSISTENCE

1. Guideline: Designers can help students to become actively engaged in a course or lesson and to persist or stay "on track" when distracted by helping them connect their personal goals and interests to course goals, by clearly communicating the utility of the course goals (and the risk of not achieving them), and by helping students maintain their confidence in achieving the course goals (by pointing out past successes with similar goals).

2. Guideline based on: Research

3. Degree of confidence: Medium

4. Comments: Clark (1999) suggested that there are three "indexes" or types of motivational goals for instruction: (1) active engagement or choice (learners actively start to do something that they formerly "intended" to do but had not started); (2) persistence (learners continue to work toward a learning or performance goal in a focused way, despite distractions); and (3) mental effort. Evidence from a number of studies supports the generalization that active engagement and persistence in distance courses are increased by two factors: value and self-efficacy (Bandura, 1997). When learners personally value what they are learning, they choose to get involved and persist over time. Active choice and persistence are also enhanced by students' beliefs that they have the ability or efficacy to learn and apply what is being taught on the job. Values include both their interest in the course objectives and the utility they associate with the benefits of finishing the course (Kanfer & McCombs, 2000).

There are suggestive indicators in existing Web-based case studies about what features students value in courses and which of those features are often missing in Web-based instruction. For example, many prospective distance learning students may be trying to overcome their perceived lack of personal contact with instructors in classroom-based courses. Students at the State University of New York who reported the highest levels of instructor interaction also reported the highest levels of value for the course (Fredericksen, Pickett, Shea, Pelz, & Swan, 2000). Thus, it seems clear that motivating distance instruction must emphasize instructor–student contact, and that this increased interaction may enhance the value of the course and therefore increase student active choice and persistence.

5. References:

Bandura, A. (1997). *Self-efficacy: The exercise of control.* New York: W. H. Freeman. [See Chapter 6, "Cognitive Functioning."]

Clark, R. E. (1999). The CaNE (Commitment and Necessary Effort) model of work motivation: A two-stage process of goal commitment and mental effort. In J. Lowyck (Ed.), *Trends in corporate training.* Leuven, Belgium: University of Leuven Press.

Fredericksen, E., Pickett, A., Shea, P., Pelz, W., & Swan, K. (2000). Student satisfaction and perceived learning with on-line courses: Principles and examples from the SUNY learning network. *Journal of Asynchronous Learner Networks, 4*(2). Retrieved June 30, 2002, from http://www.aln.org/alnweb/journal/Vol4_issue2/le/Fredericksen/LE-fredericksen.htm

Kanfer, R., & McCombs, B. L. (2000). Motivation: Applying current theory to critical issues in training. In S. Tobias & J. D. Fletcher (Eds.), *Training and retraining: A handbook for business, industry, government, and the military* (pp. 85–108). Woodbridge, CT: Macmillan Reference USA.

6. Glossary:

Self-efficacy: Self-judgment of one's ability to master a specific task and receive the support needed to accomplish it. Self-efficacy is different from "confidence." Confidence is often interpreted as a generally optimistic view of one's capabilities. Efficacy is specific to tasks and the belief that not only are we able to accomplish something, but that we will also be "permitted" and/or receive adequate support to perform the task. A person could be generally confident but have low efficacy about any given task or vice versa (Bandura, 1997).

7. User: Instructional designer

STRATEGIES BASED ON INCREASING STUDENT MOTIVATION: HELPING LEARNERS INVEST MAXIMUM MENTAL EFFORT

1. Guideline: The more that learners are convinced that the important elements of a learning task are novel to them, the more mental effort they will invest to succeed. Conversely, the more that students believe that a learning task is familiar, the more overconfident they become, the less mental effort they invest to learn, and the less they are inclined to accept responsibility for failure to learn.

2. Guideline based on: Research

3. Degree of confidence: Medium

4. Comments: Do not be misled by claims that distance learning is, by itself, motivating to students. The evidence for this claim has not been forthcoming from many studies. Salomon (1984) presented compelling contrary evidence that students who expressed a preference for learning from instruction presented via new media tended to expect that they would have to invest less effort to learn. He argued that this expectation of "easier learning" results in the investment of lower levels of mental effort by students. He provided evidence of lower achievement levels from instructional conditions that are perceived as less demanding. This finding has been replicated a number of times with different media (see, e.g., the discussion of related studies in Clark, 1999).

Clark (1999), following earlier work, suggested that there are three "indexes" or types of motivational goals for instruction: (1) active choice or commitment (learners actively start to do something that they formerly "intended" to do but had not started); (2) persistence (learners continue to work toward a learning or performance goal in a focused way, despite distractions); and (3) mental effort. Each of these types of motivational "indicators" may play a different role in, or relate differently to, the learning process in distance education.

Not much is known about the direct impact of online instructional formats on mental effort (aside from Salomon's, 1984, cautions), but the early research is not promising. Recent studies (described by Clark, 1999) indicate that many instructional strategies and complex screen displays risk overloading working memory and causing "automated" cognitive defaults where mental effort is both reduced and directed to nonlearning goals. In general, it seems that mental effort may be influenced in large part by the amount of perceived difficulty in a Web-based course (Bandura, 1997). It is possible that when moderately challenging learning goals and tasks are presented, mental effort increases. When learning tasks are perceived as too easy or impossibly difficult, mental effort decreases radically. Students seem to be able to accurately report the amount of mental effort they are investing in easy and moderately difficult tasks. Yet there is disturbing evidence that they seem unaware that they stop investing mental effort as learning tasks become extremely difficult or impossible. Designers must exercise caution not to overwhelm Web students with extremely complex tasks or screen design features that overload working memory. Meanwhile, researchers should continue to study how specific tasks and design features impact mental effort.

<table>
<tr><td>5. References:</td><td>Bandura, A. (1997). Self-efficacy: The exercise of control. New York: W. H. Freeman. [See Chapter 6, "Cognitive Functioning."]</td></tr>
</table>

5. *References:*

Bandura, A. (1997). *Self-efficacy: The exercise of control.* New York: W. H. Freeman. [See Chapter 6, "Cognitive Functioning."]

Clark, R. E. (1999). The CaNE (Commitment and Necessary Effort) model of work motivation: A two-stage process of goal commitment and mental effort. In J. Lowyck (Ed.), *Trends in corporate training.* Leuven, Belgium: University of Leuven Press.

Salomon, G. (1984). Television is "easy" and print is "tough": The differential investment of mental effort in learning as a function of perceptions and attributions. *Journal of Educational Psychology, 76,* 647–658.

6. *Glossary:*   None

7. *User:*   Instructional designer

STRATEGIES BASED ON MOTIVATING ACTIVE CHOICE TO ENGAGE IN DISTANCE LEARNING

1. *Guideline:*

Designers can help students to go beyond intention and actively choose to start a course or lesson by clearly communicating the utility of the course goals (and the risk of not achieving them), and by helping students maintain their confidence in achieving the course goals (by pointing out past successes with similar goals).

2. *Guideline based on:*   Research

3. *Degree of confidence:*   Medium

4. *Comments:*

Clark (1999) has suggested that there are three "indexes" or types of motivational goals for instruction: (1) active choice (learners actively start to do something that they formerly "intended" to do but had not started); (2) persistence (learners continue to work toward a learning or performance goal in a focused way, despite distractions); and (3) mental effort. Evidence from a number of studies supports the generalization that actively choosing to start a distance course is increased by two factors: learners' value for the content and outcome of a course (and the need to avoid the negative impact of delaying) and their specific self-efficacy for learning in the course. When learners personally value what they expect to learn, they more often decide to set aside other tasks and actively choose to start a new course or lesson. Active choice is also enhanced by students' belief that they have the ability or efficacy to learn and apply what is being taught on the job. Values include both students' interest in the course objectives and the utility students associate with the benefits of finishing the course (Kanfer & McCombs, 2000).

There are suggestive indicators in existing Web-based case studies about what features students value in courses and which of those features are often missing in Web-based instruction. For example, many prospective distance learning students may be trying to overcome their perceived lack of personal contact with instructors in classroom-based courses. Students at the State University of New York who reported the highest levels of instructor interaction also reported the highest levels of value for the online course (Fredericksen, Pickett, Shea, Pelz, & Swan, 2000). Thus, it seems clear that motivating distance instruction must emphasize synchronous and asynchronous instructor–student contact, and that the expectation of increased interaction may enhance the value of the course and therefore increase student decisions to actively choose to start the course.

5. References:

Clark, R. E. (1999). The CaNE (Commitment and Necessary Effort) model of work motivation: A two-stage process of goal commitment and mental effort. In J. Lowyck (Ed.), *Trends in corporate training.* Leuven, Belgium: University of Leuven Press.

Fredericksen, E., Pickett, A., Shea, P., Pelz, W., & Swan, K. (2000). Student satisfaction and perceived learning with on-line courses: Principles and examples from the SUNY learning network. *Journal of Asynchronous Learner Networks, 4*(2). Retrieved June 30, 2002, from http://www.aln.org/alnweb/journal/Vol4_issue2/le/Fredericksen/LE-fredericksen.htm

Kanfer, R., & McCombs, B. L. (2000). Motivation: Applying current theory to critical issues in training. In S. Tobias & J. D. Fletcher (Eds.), *Training and retraining: A handbook for business, industry, government, and the military* (pp. 85–108). Woodbridge, CT: Macmillan Reference USA.

6. Glossary: **Student interest and utility value:** Includes both students' interest in the course objectives and the utility students associate with the benefits of finishing the course (Kanfer & McCombs, 2000).

7. User: Instructional designer

STRATEGIES BASED ON MOTIVATING PERSISTENCE IN THE FACE OF DISTRACTIONS

1. Guideline: Designers can help students to persist or stay "on track" when distracted and help them maintain a positive attitude by connecting their personal goals and interests to course goals, by clearly communicating the utility of the course goals (and the risk of not achieving them), and by helping students maintain their confidence in achieving the course goals (by pointing out past successes with similar goals).

The more that instruction supports a positive attitude and maintains student interest and utility value for course goals and student self-efficacy for the course by convincing students that they are capable of achieving the learning and performance goals of the course, the more students will persist when environmental events distract them.

2. Guideline based on: Research

3. Degree of confidence: Medium

4. Comments: Clark's (1999) overview of motivation research and practice indicated that persistence in the face of distractions is one of three critical "indexes" or types of motivational problems. Evidence from a number of studies supports the generalization that persistence in distance courses is increased by three factors: mood (or attitude), value, and self-efficacy. When learners are positive and optimistic, they seem to find it easier to avoid distractions (Clark, 1999). When they personally value what they are learning (and want to avoid the negative consequence of not learning), they tend persist in a course over time, regardless of the alternative goals they consider (Kanfer & McCombs, 2000). Persistence is also enhanced by students' beliefs that they have the ability or efficacy to learn and apply what is being taught (Clark, 1999). Values include both students' interest in the course objectives and the utility students associate with the benefits of finishing the course. Clark's review of studies on persistence suggested that a positive attitude and mood can be maintained if course designers try to incorporate what learners feel are positive features such as attractive (but not distracting) graphics and animation and increased contact with trainers and instructional staff. There are suggestive indicators in existing Web-based case studies that many prospective distance learning students place a very high value on increased synchronous and asynchronous contact with trainers. Participants in a number of distance learning experiments that have the highest levels of instructor interaction also reported the highest levels of value for the course (Fredericksen, Pickett, Shea, Pelz, & Swan, 2000). Thus, it seems clear that motivating distance instruction must emphasize instructor–student contact, and that this increased interaction may enhance the value of the course and therefore increase student persistence. Finally, when students are reminded of past successes, see coping models who benefit from the learning, and receive feedback stressing the benefits of the effort they invest in learning activities, their self-efficacy for learning from a distance course tends to increase their persistence in learning activities.

5. References:

Bandura, A. (1977). Self-efficacy: Toward a unifying theory of behavioral change. *Psychological Review, 84,* 191–215.

Clark, R. E. (1999). The CaNE (Commitment and Necessary Effort) model of work motivation: A two-stage process of goal commitment and mental effort. In J. Lowyck (Ed.), *Trends in corporate training.* Leuven, Belgium: University of Leuven Press.

Fredericksen, E., Pickett, A., Shea, P., Pelz, W., & Swan, K. (2000). Student satisfaction and perceived learning with on-line courses: Principles and examples from the SUNY learning network. *Journal of Asynchronous Learner Networks, 4*(2). Retrieved June 30, 2002, from http://www.aln.org/alnweb/journal/Vol4_issue2/le/Fredericksen/LE-fredericksen.htm

Kanfer, R., & McCombs, B. L. (2000). Motivation: Applying current theory to critical issues in training. In S. Tobias & J. D. Fletcher (Eds.), *Training and retraining: A handbook for business, industry, government, and the military* (pp. 85–108). Woodbridge, CT: Macmillan Reference USA.

6. Glossary:

Student interest and utility value: Includes both students' interest in the course objectives and the utility students associate with the benefits of finishing the course (Kanfer & McCombs, 2000).

Self-efficacy: Self-judgment of one's ability to master a task. One's confidence in being able to accomplish a particular task. Self-efficacy is different from "confidence." Confidence is often interpreted as a generally optimistic view of one's capabilities. Efficacy is specific to tasks. A person could be generally confident but have low efficacy about any given task or vice versa (Bandura, 1977).

7. User:	Instructional designer

STRATEGIES BASED ON INCREASING LEARNERS' SELF-EFFICACY FOR SPECIFIC LEARNING TASKS

1. Guideline:

The more that learners believe they will be able to plan and do what is necessary to succeed on a specific learning task, the more they are motivated to begin and to persist in the face of distractions, the more eager they are to tackle a challenging task, and the more quickly they recover from learning problems, accept corrective feedback, and take responsibility for mistakes.

2. Guideline based on: Research

3. Degree of confidence: High

4. Comments:

Bandura (1997) presented overwhelming evidence for the motivational benefits of increased self-efficacy from field studies and laboratory experiments. Efficacy is a measure of our expectations that we will be able to plan and implement adequate learning strategies and achieve learning goals. People with strong self-efficacy are highly motivated to actively pursue learning goals, to persist when distracted or when they encounter difficulties, and to invest mental effort to develop effective strategies to achieve novel goals.

Clark and Estes (2002) described a number of ways to increase efficacy: (1) Provide coping models who are perceived as both effective and similar to the learner. Have models "think out loud" so that learners are able to model their thought processes as well as their behaviors. (2) Focus learning and performance feedback on people's successes, both present and past, rather than on their failures or mistakes. (3) Attribute the cause of success and mistakes to effort, not to experience, aptitude, or intelligence. Suggest that people will succeed if "you invest more effort" if they fall short of expectations, and that their success was the result of "your effort." (4) In all communication with learners, project the clear expectation that they will succeed. This includes avoiding the expression of sympathy when they fail or make mistakes. Sympathy is often interpreted as "Sorry, your best is not good enough." (5) Assign specific, short-term, and challenging learning goals. Easy goals imply a negative view of a learner's ability. Long-term, "stretch" (impossible to achieve) goals can also damage motivation.

5. References:

Bandura, A. (1997). *Self-efficacy: The exercise of control.* New York: W. H. Freeman. [See Chapter 6, "Cognitive Functioning."]

Clark, R. E., & Estes, F. (2002). *Turning research into results: A guide to selecting the right performance solution.* Atlanta, GA: CEP Press. [See Chapter 5, "Motivation Gaps: Belief Is (Almost) Everything."]

6. Glossary:

Self-efficacy: Personal belief in one's capabilities to organize and execute the courses of action required to produce given attainments (Bandura, 1997). Self-efficacy is different from "confidence." Confidence is often interpreted as a generally optimistic view of one's capabilities. Efficacy is specific to tasks. A person could be generally confident but have low efficacy about any given task or vice versa.

7. User:

Instructional designer

STRATEGIES BASED ON DECREASING LEARNER PROCRASTINATION

1. Guideline: Learners who delay starting until the last minute and/or are easily distracted and so interrupt the flow of their learning until it is too late to do a good job learn much less, and are less effective at transferring what they have learned to the job after training.

2. Guideline based on: Research

3. Degree of confidence: Medium

4. Comments: Procrastinators use a variety of devices to delay working on a task. Some of these strategies are very sophisticated and difficult to identify and so procrastinators are sometimes labeled as "slow learners." Wolters (2003) described the characteristics of learners who may become procrastinators in two studies with college-age populations. The characteristics include (a) learners with low self-efficacy for the specific learning goals; (b) a lack of value for the learning goals (including a lack of utility value for achieving the goals); and (c) the desire to avoid failure by avoiding challenging tasks (work avoidance). In addition, many procrastinators have inadequate study and time management skills and tend to have more test anxiety and to seek help less often. In general, it appears that lower self-efficacy and lower value for learning goals tend to produce or increase emotional distress, which leads to lowered impulse control and subsequent giving in to the immediate gratification that results from not investing effort on learning tasks.

Clark (2003) and Wolters (2003) described a number of ways to overcome procrastination: (1) Assess learners' self-efficacy and, if it is below average, provide supportive feedback based on their positive accomplishments, increase their efficacy, and avoid negative feedback or focusing on learners' mistakes (see self-efficacy discussion). (2) Determine learners' values and connect their personal values with the learning task (including the utility of completing the task and the risk of doing poorly on it). (3) Help learners maintain a positive mood during learning to dispel their impulsive need to feel good by avoiding learning tasks (see positive attitude strategies). (4) Avoid permitting "learner control" over when students must study and practice what they are learning. Build into each course mandated completion schedules, learning plans, self-assessments, and time management strategies.

5. References:

Clark, R. E. (2003). Fostering the work motivation of individuals and teams. *Performance Improvement, 42*(3), 21–29.

Kanfer, R., & McCombs, B. L. (2000). Motivation: Applying current theory to critical issues in training. In S. Tobias & J. D. Fletcher (Eds.), *Training and retraining: A handbook for business, industry, government, and the military* (pp. 85–108). Woodbridge CT: Macmillan Reference USA.

Wolters, C. A. (2003). Understanding procrastination from a self-regulated learning perspective. *Journal of Educational Psychology, 95,* 179–187.

6. Glossary:

Procrastination: Failing to achieve learning goals within a desired or mandated time frame and/or postponing until the last minute activities one ultimately intends to complete to the point where the learner experiences emotional distress and the quality and quantity of learning is significantly decreased (Wolters, 2003).

Self-efficacy: Self-judgment of one's ability to master a specific task and receive the support needed to accomplish it. Self-efficacy is different from "confidence." Confidence is often interpreted as a generally optimistic view of one's capabilities. Efficacy is specific to tasks and the belief that not only are we able to accomplish something, but that we will also be "permitted" and/or receive adequate support to perform the task. A person could be generally confident but have low efficacy about any given task or vice versa (Bandura, 1997).

Student utility value: Student utility value includes both students' interest in the course objectives and the utility students associate with the benefits of finishing the course (Kanfer & McCombs, 2000).

7. User: Instructional designer

STRATEGIES BASED ON MOTIVATING LEARNERS BY INCREASING THE VALUE OF LEARNING GOALS AND OBJECTIVES

1. Guideline: The more that instruction connects learner interest, utility, and skill values with course goals, the more motivated learners will be to learn during distance learning and to transfer what they have learned back to their jobs after training.

2. Guideline based on: Research

3. Degree of confidence: Medium

4. Comments: Eccles and Wigfield (2002), Kanfer and McCombs (2000), and Higgins (2000) have argued persuasively that our values exert a major influence on our decisions to engage in activities and persist at them in the face of distractions. Motivation researchers suggest that values combine with expectancies for success (self-efficacy) to determine what we will choose to do. When we value an activity and believe that we can succeed, we are more likely to pursue that activity. Eccles and Wigfield (2002) have described four types of values that are most often used by people when deciding about whether they will persist at learning or avoid it in favor of a more appealing set of tasks. Those four types are (1) attainment value—the perception that a learning task reflects what we believe to be our personal strengths and our view of ourselves; (2) intrinsic value—which characterizes learning experiences that we like and enjoy and/or that interest us; (3) utility value—which is determined by how much a learning task facilitates important career goals or has attractive qualities apart from what is learned; and (4) cost—which is a measure of both the expected effort and the lost opportunities one experiences when making a commitment to work on a distance course.

Supporting learners' value for a distance learning course requires creative ways to support all four of the types of values. The first suggestion is that designers follow the old principle, "If it's not broken, don't fix it." Designers are advised not to try to add to the value learners have for distance courses if students have already started and are working consistently and effectively. There is evidence that trying to increase the motivation of already adequately motivated people can backfire under some conditions. However, if learners are avoiding starting a course or if computer-use statistics indicate that they are not logging on and working consistently, try using Eccles and Wigfield's (2002) four types of values as a way to encourage them to start something or persist at learning. In order to establish attainment value, use a "Try it, you are good at this kind of task" message. For intrinsic interest value, use the "This is the kind of class you might like—it will give you another set of skills" approach, and give examples from their past accomplishments. Utility value is reflected in the message "Even if you don't like the idea of working on this course, think of the benefits of finishing it (or related benefits) and also think of the risks you take if you do not finish it." Finally, cost–benefit decisions are captured in the message that "This course will give you much more benefit than the things you are doing to avoid it."

5. References:	Eccles, J., & Wigfield, A. (2002). Motivational beliefs, values and goals. *Annual Review of Psychology, 53,* 109–132.
	Higgins, E. T. (2000). Making a good decision: Value from fit. *American Psychologist, 55,* 1217–1230.
	Kanfer, R., & McCombs, B. L. (2000). Motivation: Applying current theory to critical issues in training. In S. Tobias & J. D. Fletcher (Eds.), *Training and retraining: A handbook for business, industry, government, and the military* (pp. 85–108). Woodbridge CT: Macmillan Reference USA.
6. Glossary:	None
7. User:	Instructional designer

STRATEGIES BASED ON THE MOTIVATIONAL IMPACT OF EFFECTIVE INSTRUCTIONAL MODELS

1. Guideline:	Designers can increase learner motivation by selecting people to model behavior, or to be "onscreen" teachers or demonstrators, who are perceived by learners as competent, similar (to the learners in that they "cope" with adversity well), and are credible and enthusiastic.
2. Guideline based on:	Research
3. Degree of confidence:	Medium
4. Comments:	When a distance learning course design calls for the use of "on-camera" or "in-person" demonstrations by trainers and/or experts, Bandura (1997) made a strong case for selecting people who have four qualities (as perceived by the learners): (1) competence, (2) similarity (to the learners), (3) credibility, and (4) enthusiasm. In a number of studies described by Bandura, competence was judged to be a more important attribute of a model than age, gender, or culture. Models who are perceived as competent command more attention and exert greater

instructional influence. Similarity of the model to the learners is important when the skill being modeled touches on gender, age, or culturally specific tasks. For example, a nonathletic woman successfully modeling a technique for physical conditioning is perceived as more motivating than an athletic man performing the same task. Another feature of credibility in models is whether they exhibit a "coping" style. That is, the behavior of models should not always be "perfect." When models represent "novices" who are learning something (such as the nonathletic woman practicing a conditioning task), make some mistakes, and need feedback to correct them, they are more motivating than models who only exhibit "perfection." Learners are also persuaded more by models they judge to be credible. Bandura argued that models perceived as credible not only tend to have solid experience in the task being learned, but also are viewed as skilled in knowing how to teach it. Finally, to support a positive attitude and mood, models who are positive and enthusiastic are more motivating than people who are bland or negative (Pintrich, 2003).

Research on the motivational qualities of models has been independently confirmed by Lockwood, Jordan, and Kunda (2002), whose studies support the conclusion that learners tend to value both "promotion" (work to succeed) and "prevention" (work to avoid failure) goals as they learn. Coping models who are perceived as similar to the learners fit the prevention style. Competent, credible, and enthusiastic models support the promotion style. Lockwood and colleagues made the point that all of us use both types of goals to succeed, and therefore both types and styles of models are motivating.

5. References:

Bandura, A. (1997). *Self-efficacy: The exercise of control.* New York: W. H. Freeman. [See Chapter 3, "Sources of Efficacy."]

Lockwood, P., Jordan, C. H., & Kunda, Z.
(2002). Motivation by positive or negative
role models: Regulatory focus determines
who will best inspire us. *Journal of Personality
and Social Psychology, 83,* 854–864.

Pintrich, P. R. (2003). A motivational science
perspective on the role of student motivation in learning and teaching contexts. *Journal of Educational Psychology, 95,* 667–686.

6. Glossary: None

7. User: Instructional designer

STRATEGIES BASED ON THE MOTIVATIONAL IMPACT OF EFFECTIVE PERFORMANCE ATTRIBUTIONS

1. Guideline: When learners experience negative, unexpected, or novel problems during learning, they
are more motivated to persist and invest mental
effort in correcting the problems if feedback
attributes the cause to personally controllable
factors such as a defective learning or problem-
solving strategy that can be remedied with effort
on the part of the learner and support from an
instructor or help menu.

2. Guideline based on: Research

3. Degree of confidence: Medium

4. Comments: Weiner (1991) was the first to present compelling evidence that nearly everyone searches for
the causes of negative, unexpected, or novel
events. His "attribution [perceived causes] theory" of motivation suggests that our reasons or
causes for success and/or failure have a major
impact on our present and future learning. His
advice to instructional designers and instructors
was to attribute success and failure to causes that
were within the control of the student (e.g.,
effort or learning strategies). When learners succeed, effort and strategy feedback gives them
information supporting their hard work and use

of effective strategies. When they fail to achieve goals, attributing the failure to a correctable strategy and urging more effort places the solution under the learner's control (Försterling, 2001). Bandura and Locke (2003), two giants in motivation research, jointly and recently reinforced this claim by urging educators at all levels to stress learners' control over all of their accomplishments, including mistakes and failures to achieve their goals. They recommended that information given to learners about their progress point out what they have accomplished in very accurate and positive language and attribute their success to effort. For example, if a learner accomplishes 75% of a learning goal in a distance learning module, emphasize the significant progress toward the goal (the 75%) and not the gap (the 25%). When learners fail to achieve a goal, Bandura and Locke recommended that the most motivational feedback is an analysis of how the learner's strategy could be adjusted to achieve the learning goal. Designers should provide help so that the learner can develop a more effective learning strategy. This design strategy shifts the cause of the failure from something uncontrollable in the student (a lack of ability) to a controllable cause (an improvable learning or problem-solving strategy). Bandura and Locke most specifically argued against telling learners "You have failed to achieve…" or "You made X number of errors/mistakes." Pointing out the fact that a person "committed" a mistake or error focuses attention on a lack of ability and decreases self-efficacy. It makes an issue of the learner and not the learning.

5. References:

Bandura, A., & Locke, E. A. (2003). Negative self-efficacy and goal effects revisited. *Journal of Applied Psychology, 88,* 87–99.

Försterling, F. (2001). *Attribution: An introduction to theories, research and applications.* Philadelphia: Taylor & Francis. [See Chapter 1, "The Topics of Attribution Research."]

Weiner, B. (1991). Metaphors in motivation and attribution. *American Psychologist, 46,* 921–930.

6. Glossary: None

7. User: Instructional designer

CHAPTER 7

SELF-REGULATION
STRATEGIES

Harold F. O'Neil and Sanhui (Sabrina) Chuang
University of Southern California/CRESST

The following guidelines are presented in this chapter:

Strategies Based on Goal Specificity
Strategies Based on Setting Process and Outcome Goals
Strategies Based on Self-Evaluation
Strategies Based on Self-Monitoring
Strategies Based on Self-Questioning
Strategies Based on Effort Allocation

STRATEGIES BASED ON GOAL SPECIFICITY

1. Guideline: Learners learn better with specific performance standards than with general standards
such as "Do your best."

2. Guideline based on: Research

What Works in Distance Learning: Guidlines, pages 111–121
Copyright © 2005 by Information Age Publishing
All rights of reproduction in any form reserved.

3. Degree of confidence: High

4. Comments: Specific performance standards in a task provide learners an easy way to determine how much effort and time are needed to complete the task. Therefore, goal specificity provides learners a better chance of achieving the goal. After the task is completed, learners will experience a sense of satisfaction, which leads to higher self-efficacy.

According to the literature, the more specific the performance goal standards are in a task, the easier it is for learners to determine how much effort is needed in order to complete the task. Task specificity is more likely to increase self-regulated learning than goals that say "Do your best."

In addition, goal specificity increases commitment on the task. Furthermore, the specificity of a goal also leads to higher self-efficacy because it is easier to evaluate the required learning progress when the goal is specific than when it is vague. With goal specificity, it is also easier for the instructional designer to design feedback for learners (Locke & Latham, 2002; Schunk, 2003; Wright & Kacmar, 1994).

In an online learning setting, instructional designers should try to specify as much detail as possible as to what exactly learners need to learn so that they can easily evaluate their own learning progress.

5. References: Bandura, A. (1977). Self-efficacy: Toward a unifying theory of behavioral change. *Psychological Review, 84,* 191–215.

Locke, E. A., & Latham, G. P. (2002). Building a practically useful theory of goal setting and task motivation. *American Psychologist, 57,* 705–717.

Schunk, D. H. (2003). Self-efficacy for reading and writing: Influence of modeling, goal setting and self-evaluation. *Reading and Writing Quarterly, 19,* 159–172.

Wright, P. M., & Kacmar, K. M. (1994). Goal specificity as a determinant of goal commitment and goal change. *Organizational Behavior and Human Decision Processes, 59*, 242–260.

6. Glossary:	**Self-efficacy:** Self-judgment of one's ability to master a task. One's confidence in being able to accomplish a particular task (Bandura, 1977).
	Task specificity: Task with specific performance standards against which learners can evaluate their progress on the task (Schunk, 2003).
7. User:	Instructional designer

STRATEGIES BASED ON SETTING PROCESS AND OUTCOME GOALS

1. Guideline:	Students who set process goals initially and then shift to outcome goals learn better than those who adhere to process goals only; in addition, students who adhere to process goals only learn better than those who adhere to outcome goals only.
2. Guideline based on:	Research
3. Degree of confidence:	High
4. Comments:	Self-regulated learners plan, set goals, and monitor and evaluate their learning. Specifically, within goal setting, research has shown that learners who shift goals from process to outcome goals perform better than students who adhere to process goals only or to outcome goals only (Zimmerman & Kitsantas, 1997).

According to the literature, there are three ways self-regulated learning can be taught to learners: (1) indirectly, through their experience; (2) directly, through instruction; and (3) elicited through practice (Paris & Paris, 2001). It is therefore possible to teach self-regulation to learners in a distance learning setting. Instructors can provide explicit instruction about self-regulated learning to help students become more self-regulated learners.

Thus, in a distance learning setting, instruction should include explanations for the need to set both process goals and outcome goals. For instance, state that setting process goals and outcome goals is beneficial to successfully accomplishing a task, and that learners can set process goals to check their performance in each step of their learning and set outcome goals that summarize all the learning results. An example of a process goal in chemistry would be to learn the chemical elements presented in each lesson. An example of an outcome goal would be to have learned all the chemical elements and to know their relationship to one another.

5. References:

Locke, E. A., & Latham, G. P. (2002). Building a practically useful theory of goal setting and task motivation: A 35-year odyssey. *American Psychologist, 57,* 705–717.

Paris, G. S., & Paris, H. A. (2001). Classroom applications of research on self-regulated learning. *Educational Psychologist, 52,* 267–306.

Zimmerman, B. J., & Kitsantas, A. (1997). Developmental phases in self-regulation: Shifting from process goals to outcome goals. *Journal of Educational Psychology, 89,* 29–36.

6. Glossary:

Goal setting: Establishing quantitative or qualitative standards of performance (Locke & Latham, 2002).

Outcome goals: End goals that summarize all the learning results (Zimmerman & Kitsantas, 1997).

Process goals: Proximal goals that learners use to check their performance in each process of their learning (Zimmerman & Kitsantas, 1997).

Self-regulated learning: Learning in which learners plan, set goals, and monitor and evaluate their learning (Zimmerman & Kitsantas, 1997).

7. User:

Instructional designer

STRATEGIES BASED ON SELF-EVALUATION

1. Guideline: Students who self-evaluate their learning results regularly and are conscious of their own progress and performance in learning perform better academically than those who do not.

2. Guideline based on: Research

3. Degree of confidence: High

4. Comments: Self-regulated learners plan, set goals, and monitor and evaluate their learning. However, research has shown that many learners do not self-evaluate their learning results and progress automatically. Self-evaluation is important to self-regulation. Students who self-evaluate their learning perform better academically (Ley & Young, 2001; Schunk, 2003).

Self-evaluations also raise self-efficacy because learners become consciously aware of what they have been doing, which results in satisfactory performance. Low self-evaluations do not always decrease self-efficacy as long as learners have the options or skills to use alternative methods to accomplish the task (Walker, 2003).

For learners who are not spontaneous and skillful in their self-evaluation, instructional designers should include opportunities for learners to reflect on and evaluate their learning results and performance. Schunk (2003) suggested using a self-evaluation report scale on which learners rate their own learning progress as a method for teaching this self-evaluation strategy. Walker (2003) suggested a teacher-prepared checklist for students to use to evaluate their learning when they have completed their specific tasks.

5. References: Ley, K., & Young B. D. (2001). Instructional principles for self-regulation. *Educational Technology Research and Development, 49*(2), 93–103.

O'Neil, H. F., Jr., & Abedi, J. (1996). Reliability and validity of a state metacognitive inventory: Potential for alternative assessment. *Journal of Educational Research, 89,* 234–245.

Schunk, D. H. (2003). Self-efficacy for reading and writing: Influence of modeling, goal setting and self-evaluation. *Reading and Writing Quarterly, 19,* 159–172.

Walker, B. J. (2003). The cultivation of student self-efficacy in reading and writing. *Reading and Writing Quarterly, 19,* 173–187.

6. Glossary: **Self-evaluation:** A self-comparison between some component of performance and the set standard (O'Neil & Abedi, 1996).

7. User: Instructional designer

STRATEGIES BASED ON SELF-MONITORING

1. Guideline: Students who periodically monitor their own learning progress by checking what they know and don't know perform better academically than those who do not make an effort to monitor their own learning.

2. Guideline based on: Research

3. Degree of confidence: High

4. Comments: Self-regulated learners plan, set goals, and monitor and evaluate their learning. Self-regulation is composed of metacognition (planning and self-monitoring) and motivation (effort and self-efficacy) (O'Neil & Abedi, 1996). Most definitions of self-regulation include a self-oriented feedback loop, which refers to a cyclic process in which students monitor their own learning performance and respond to self-generated feedback through overt changes in their behavior. Thus self-monitoring is central to self-regulation. The literature indicates that students who self-monitor their learning perform better academically (Ley & Young, 1998). In a study by Lan (1996), learners who recorded their learning progress on a self-monitoring protocol scored higher than learners who did not record their progress. The extra feedback provided by learners in this study resulted in improved learning outcomes.

Zimmerman (2000) stated that self-monitoring skills can be taught as a cognitive skill in four phases: (1) baseline self-monitoring, which collects initial data about the academic activity; (2) structured self-monitoring, in which students self-observe according to a structured monitoring protocol; (3) independent self-monitoring, in which students adapt the course-related self-monitoring protocol to their needs; and (4) self-regulated self-monitoring, in which students develop monitoring protocols for other academic activities on their own.

Therefore, in an online learning setting, instructional designers can help learners to become more skilled in self-monitoring by providing opportunities for learners to monitor their own progress and performance. The self-monitoring instruction should include prompts for learners to observe and record what they do and do not do as they learn.

5. References:

Lan, W. Y. (1996). The effects of self-monitoring on students' course performance, use of learning strategies, attitude, self-judgment ability, and knowledge representation. *Journal of Experimental Education, 64,* 101–115.

Ley, K., & Young, D. B. (1998). Self-regulation behaviors in underprepared (developmental) and regular admission college students. *Contemporary Educational Psychology, 23,* 42–64.

O'Neil, H. F., Jr., & Abedi, J. (1996). Reliability and validity of a state metacognitive inventory: Potential for alternative assessment. *Journal of Educational Research, 89,* 234–245.

Zimmerman, B. J. (2000). Self-efficacy: An essential motive to learn. *Contemporary Educational Psychology, 25,* 82–91.

Zimmerman, B. J., & Kitsantas, A. (1997). Developmental phases in self-regulation: Shifting from process to outcome goals. *Journal of Educational Psychology, 89,* 29–36.

6. Glossary: **Metacognition:** Conscious and periodic self-checking of whether one's goal is achieved and, when necessary, selecting and applying different strategies (O'Neil & Abedi, 1996).

Self-monitoring: A self-checking mechanism to monitor goal achievement (O'Neil & Abedi, 1996).

Self-regulated learning: Learning in which learners plan, set goals, and monitor and evaluate their learning (Zimmerman & Kitsantas, 1997).

7. User: Instructional designer

STRATEGIES BASED ON SELF-QUESTIONING

1. Guideline: Learners who question themselves about the learning content while learning perform better academically than those who do not.

2. Guideline based on: Research

3. Degree of confidence: High

4. Comments: Self-questioning (a form of self-monitoring) provides a chance for learners to really know how much they have already learned and what they need to spend more time on (Zimmerman, 1995). In addition, when learners question themselves about what they have learned and they are able to answer questions they have developed, they will have a sense of achievement and, in turn, will be more willing to continue learning. On other hand, when learners are unable to answer the questions they have developed for themselves, they need to change their way of learning so that they will be more successful.

Research has shown that in reading and in computer-assisted problem-solving tasks, learners who use a self-questioning strategy to guide their understanding of learned material have higher achievement than learners who use instructor-provided questions or learners who use no questions at all. The literature suggests that by developing questions themselves, learners have to elaborate their own thinking about the materials, thus enhancing their learning (King, 1991, 1994a, 1994b).

In a distance learning setting, instructional designers should include a mechanism for learners to reflect on their learning. One way is to have learners ask themselves questions about the content of the materials. The instructional designer can provide hints for developing questions or provide sample questions. In addition, the designer should also provide learners with a mechanism for answering and checking their answers to their own questions. If possible, feedback should be provided according to learners' responses to the questions.

5. References:

King, A. (1991). Improving lecture comprehension: Effects of a metacognitive strategy. *Applied Cognitive Psychology, 5*, 331–346.

King, A. (1994a). Autonomy and question asking: The role of personal control in guided student-generated questioning. *Learning and Individual Differences, 6*, 163–185.

King, A. (1994b). Guiding knowledge construction in the classroom: Effects of teaching children how to question and how to explain. *American Educational Research Journal, 31*, 338–368.

Zimmerman, J. B. (1995). Self-monitoring during collegiate studying: An invaluable tool for academic self-regulation. *New Directions for Teaching and Learning, 63*, 13–27.

6. Glossary:

Self-questioning: A strategy learners use by asking or generating questions about the learning content and answering those questions on their own (King, 1994a, 1994b).

7. User:

Instructional designer

STRATEGIES BASED ON EFFORT ALLOCATION

1. Guideline:

Self-regulated learners strategically allocate effort according to what they know and what they do not know about the content to be learned. They learn better because effort allocation gives learners a chance to evaluate what they know or do not know and, in addition, possibly change their allocation of effort if necessary after a period of time at the task.

2. Guideline based on: Research

3. Degree of confidence: High

4. Comments:

Something that distinguishes a self-regulated learner from a non-self-regulated learner is that self-regulated learners know how to allocate their effort so that increased learning will follow. Self-regulated learners strategically allocate effort according to what they know and what they do not know about the content to be learned.

Evaluating what they know and do not know about the content to be learned and understanding the key points gives learners a chance to evaluate whether their original effort allocation is efficient and effective. Learners should want to change their allocation of effort if the original allocation is not the most desirable. However, research has shown that most learners do not spontaneously exercise effort allocation when they learn unless they are explicitly instructed and encouraged to do so by the design of the learning materials (Lin & Lehman, 1999).

Therefore, it is important in a distance learning setting for instructional designers to provide frequent chances for learners to first examine their understanding of the content and second, explain specifically both what they know and what they do not know about the content. Asking learners to explain what they know and do not know helps learners determine why they learn well and do not learn well (Lin & Lehman, 1999; Paris & Paris, 2001).

When learners engage in the kinds of self-regulated learning activities mentioned above, they become consciously aware of their learning process. This results in reexamination of their effort reallocation. Learners realize either that their effort allocation is good and results in effective understanding of the materials, or that effort reallocation is necessary in order to achieve the desired level of learning. When learners are aware of their own learning and effort allocation, they are more confident (Zimmerman, 1998).

5. References:

Lin, X., & Lehman, J. (1999). Supporting learning of variable control in a computer-based biology environment: Effects of prompting college students to reflect on their own thinking. *Journal of Research in Science Teaching, 36,* 837–858.

Paris, G. S., & Paris, H. A. (2001). Classroom applications of research on self-regulated learning. *Educational Psychologist, 52,* 267–306.

Zimmerman, B. J. (1998). Academic studying and the development of personal skill: A self-regulatory perspective. *Educational Psychologist, 33*(2/3), 73–86.

Zimmerman, B. J., & Kitsantas, A. (1997). Developmental phases in self-regulation: Shifting from process goals to outcome goals. *Journal of Educational Psychology, 89,* 29–36.

6. Glossary:

Effort allocation: Where and how a learner divides his or her limit of effort to achieve a learning goal (Zimmerman, 1998).

Self-regulated learning: Learning in which learners plan, set goals, and monitor and evaluate their learning (Zimmerman & Kitsantas, 1997).

7. User:

Instructional designer

CHAPTER 8

MANAGEMENT STRATEGIES

Edward Kazlauskas
University of Southern California

The following guidelines are presented in this chapter:

Strategies Based on Policy Framework and Administrative Structure
Strategies Based on Technical Support Environment
Strategies Based on Quality Assurance
Strategies Based on Library and Information Systems and Services
Strategies Based on Content Management Systems
Strategies Based on Student Support Services
Strategies Based on Instructor Competency
Strategies Based on Learner Characteristics
Strategies Based on Instructional Design

What Works in Distance Learning: Guidlines, pages 123–141
Copyright © 2005 by Information Age Publishing
All rights of reproduction in any form reserved.

STRATEGIES BASED ON POLICY FRAMEWORK AND ADMINISTRATIVE STRUCTURE

1. Guideline: A policy framework, administrative structure, and appropriate procedures and interventions should be developed to support distance learning efforts.

2. Guideline based on: Expert opinion

3. Degree of confidence: Medium

4. Comments: Considerable effort has been placed on identifying the barriers to successful distance training and education. For example, Muilenburg and Berge (2001) identified barriers to distance education such as technical expertise, support, and infrastructure; evaluation and effectiveness; and faculty compensation and time. Many of the constructs identified by these researchers relate to a management perspective, that is, the need for an adequate administrative structure and for organizational change. There is a need for management that supports distance learning efforts with commitment, a supportive organizational structure, and appropriate policy development. To overcome the barriers to distance learning, provide a shared vision for distance learning, develop a strategic plan, activate an organizational structure that supports distance learning, and implement appropriate policies and procedures.

From another perspective, Prestera and Moller (2001) applied human performance technology to organizational alignment for distance learning efforts, with attention to developing the goals, structure, and management practices associated with distance education programs.

5. References: Bunn, M. D. (2001). Timeless and timely issues in distance education planning. *American Journal of Distance Education, 13*(1), 55–67.
Cho, S. K., & Berge, Z. L. (2002). Overcoming barriers to distance training and education. *United States Distance Learning Association Journal, 16*(1). Retrieved July 11, 2002, from

http://www.usdla.org/html/journal/
JAN02_Issue/article01.html
International Society for Performance Improvement (ISPI). (n.d.). *What is HPT?* Retrieved July 18, 2002, from http://www.ispi.org/
hpt_institute/
Joint Committee on Standards for Educational Evaluation. (1994). *Program evaluation standards* (2nd ed.). Thousand Oaks, CA: Sage. (See also *Glossary of evaluation terms.* Kalamazoo: Western Michigan University, Evaluation Center. Retrieved July 18, 2002, from http://ec.wmich.edu/glossary)
Muilenburg, L. Y., & Berge, Z. L (2001). Barriers to distance education: A factor analytic study. *American Journal of Distance Education, 13*(2), 7–22.
Prestera, G. E., & Moller, L. A. (2001). Organizational alignment supporting distance education in post-secondary institutions. *Online Journal of Distance Learning Administration, 4*(4). Retrieved July 18, 2002, from http://www.westga.edu/~distance/ojdla/winter44/prestera44.html

6. Glossary: **Human performance technology:** A set of methods and procedures, and a strategy for solving problems, for realizing opportunities related to the performance of people. Human performance technology can be applied to individuals, small groups, and large organizations. It is, in reality, a systematic combination of three fundamental processes: performance analysis, cause analysis, and intervention selection (ISPI, n.d.).

7. User: Program manager

STRATEGIES BASED ON TECHNICAL SUPPORT
ENVIRONMENT

1. Guideline: Provide the technical framework, hardware and software, and technical support for the distance learning constituency (e.g., designers, trainers, and learners).

2. Guideline based on: Expert opinion

3. Degree of confidence: Medium

4. Comments: Common among successful organizations is an e-learning strategy that focuses on infrastructure with components therein focusing on technical architecture, standards for integrating existing and future online learning elements, and matching content to delivery whether that be Web-based training (WBT), interactive TV, or other technologies (McGraw, 2001).

           Reports from a variety of organizational contexts document the need to build quality distance learning programs, with technology as a component of various general-purpose distance learning checklists that indicate the various factors that should be considered (Western Interstate Commission for Higher Education, 2001). Some specific examples of components include integrity and validity of information; interactivity; information presentation, learning space activity, system reliability, security, and system support; and upgrades/improvements. A major aspect of developing the technical support environment is the conscious effort of selecting a learning management system. Using the results from survey research of 112 suppliers of learning management systems, Hall (2000) presented a bottom-line list of elements to be considered, including functionality, ease of use, integration, and standards compliance.

5. References: Hall, B. (2000). LMS 2001. *Learning circuits.* Alexandria, VA: American Society for Training and Development. Retrieved July 20, 2002, from http://www.learningcircuits.org/2001/jan2001/hall.html [See also 21-page executive summary of a full, extensive report: Hall, B. (2002). *Learning management systems 2002.* Sunnyvale, CA: brandon-hall.com. Retrieved July 20, 2002, from http://www.brandonhall.com/public/ execsums/execsum_LMS2002]

McGraw, K. L. (2001). E-learning strategy equals infrastructure. *Learning circuits.* Alexandria, VA: American Society for Training and Development. Retrieved July 20, 2002, from http://www.learningcircuits.org/2001/ jube2001/mcgraw.html

Western Interstate Commission for Higher Education—WICHE. (2001). *Best-practices for electronically offered degree and certificate programs.* Boulder, CO: Author. Retrieved July 20, 2002, from http://www.wiche.edu/telecom/Accrediting-BestPractices.pdf

6. Glossary: **WBT:** Web-based training; delivery of educational content via a Web browser. WBT often provides links to other learning resources and discussion groups and may include a facilitator who can provide course guidelines, manage discussion boards, and deliver lectures. [American Society for Training and Development. (n.d.). Glossary (compiled by E. Kaplan-Leiserson). *Learning circuits.* Alexandria, VA: Author. Retrieved July 20, 2002, from http://www.learningcircuits.org/glossary.html]

7. User: Program manager

STRATEGIES BASED ON QUALITY ASSURANCE

1. Guideline: Quality assurance for a distance education service is provided through the specification of standards in such areas as organizational support, course development, teaching/learning, course structure, student support, instructor support, and evaluation/assessment, and through steps taken to ensure that the standards are met.

2. Guideline based on: Expert opinion

3. Degree of confidence: Medium

4. Comments: In a report on benchmarks for success in Internet based distance education (Phipps & Merisoitis, 2000), six institutions were examined that are leaders in distance education to ascertain their level of compliance with quality standards identified and published by various entities. The report outlined 24 benchmarks considered to be essential for quality distance education programs, covering the areas of organizational support, course development, the teaching/learning process, course structure, student support, instructor support, and evaluation/assessment.

Quality assurance has more of a business orientation when compared to the traditional education model. Pond (2002) discussed the paradigm shift associated with this approach, with, for example, a change from institution-focused to learner-focused benchmarks for success, and from a process-based model to a product/outcome-based model.

Included in distance education quality assurance is, in implementing general ISO 9001:2000 *Standards for Quality Management Systems,* a quality assurance model with 20 sets of system requirements, many of which are technology-related, that can act as a guide and assist in Quality Assurance Certification (Benjamin Franklin Institute of Global Education, 2001).

5. References: Benjamin Franklin Institute of Global Education. (2001). *Distance education—Quality Assurance Institute.* San Diego, CA: Author. Retrieved July 20, 2002, from http//www.academyweb.com/depaintro.htm

Phipps, R., & Merisoitis, J. (2000). *Quality on the line: Benchmarks for success in Internet-based dis-*

tance education. Washington DC: Institute for Higher Education Policy.

Pond, W. K. (2002). Distributed education in the 21st century: Implications for quality assurance. *Online Journal of Distance Learning Administration, 5*(2). Retrieved July 20, 2002, from http://www.westga.edu/~distance/ojdla/summer52/pond52.html

6. *Glossary:*   **ISO 9001:** International Organization for Standardization; an international federation of national standards bodies. Standards relating to quality assurance. [American Society for Training and Development. (n.d.). Glossary (compiled by E. Kaplan-Leiserson). *Learning circuits.* Alexandria, VA: Author. Retrieved July 20, 2002, from http://www.learningcircuits.org/glossary.html]

7. *User:*   Program manager

STRATEGIES BASED ON LIBRARY AND INFORMATION SYSTEMS AND SERVICES

1. *Guideline:*   For a distance learning program to succeed there must be appropriate library and information systems and services.

2. *Guideline based on:*   Expert opinion

3. *Degree of confidence:*   Medium

4. *Comments:*   Traditionally the library has been the vehicle that has supported student learning through access to resources, assistance in the search for such resources, and retrieval of materials. Recently, the library has transformed itself into a digital repository with additional resources, including full text, made available over the World Wide Web. It is incumbent on distance learning management to provide for such access and use, either through existing library services or through contract with library-service providers. Library-related organizations, such as the American Library Association, have developed guidelines for distance learning library services (Association of College and Research Libraries, 2000). Most distance learning evaluation guidelines, such as that from the Western Interstate Commission for Higher Education (2001), include library/information resources as a criterion.

In a report for a major bibliographic utility, McLean (2002) noted the need for interoperability/interaction of traditional library systems with the new concept of "learning space." Included in this concept is the interplay of internal document and content management systems, online search and retrieval systems, external resources, and portals.

5. References:

Association of College and Research Libraries. (2000). *Guidelines for distance learning library services.* Chicago: American Library Association. Retrieved July 20, 2002, from http://www.ala.org/acrl/guides/distlrng.html

McLean, N. (2002). *Libraries and e-learning: Organizational and technical interoperability.* Dublin, OH: Online Computer Library Center. Retrieved July 20, 2002, from http://www.oclc.org/research/publications/archive/mclean_neil_2002000308_rev.doc

Western Interstate Commission for Higher Education—WICHE. (2001). *Best practices for electronically offered degree and certificate programs.* Boulder, CO: Author. Retrieved July 20, 2002, from http://www.wiche.edu/telecom/Accrediting-BestPractices.pdf

6. Glossary:

Content management system (CMS) or Learning content management system (LCMS): A software application that allows trainers and training directors to manage both the administrative and content-related functions of training. An LCMS combines the course management capabilities of an LMS (learning management system) with the content creation and storage capabilities of a CMS (content management system).

Includes learning objects, the reusable, media-independent chunks of information used as modular building blocks for e-learning content. [American Society for Training and Development. (n.d.). Glossary (compiled by E. Kaplan-Leiserson). *Learning circuits.* Alexandria, VA: Author. Retrieved July 20, 2002, from http://www.learningcircuits.org/glossary.html]

Learning space: An imaginary geography in which the learning enterprise flourishes. [American Society for Training and Development. (n.d.). Glossary (compiled by E. Kaplan-Leiserson). *Learning circuits.* Alexandria, VA: Author. Retrieved July 20, 2002, from http://www.learningcircuits.org/glossary.html]

Portal: A Web site that acts as a "doorway" to the Internet, or a portion of the Internet, targeted toward one particular subject; offers learners or organizations consolidated access to learning and training resourses from multiple sources. [American Society for Training and Development. (n.d.). Glossary (compiled by E. Kaplan-Leiserson). *Learning circuits.* Alexandria, VA: Author. Retrieved July 20, 2002, from http://www.learningcircuits.org/glossary.html]

7. User:	Program manager

STRATEGIES BASED ON CONTENT MANAGEMENT SYSTEMS

1. Guideline:	Monitor and be proactive regarding the developments in content management and in reuse and interoperation among learning systems.
2. Guideline based on:	Expert opinion
3. Degree of confidence:	Medium
4. Comments:	To exploit the cost benefits and return on investment of distance learning, an approach is needed that will easily create, rapidly deploy, and manage content. A learning content man-

agement system (LCMS) provides for the management of the administrative functions of training and, importantly, for the management of the learning content in the form of small learning objects, in effect separating the content from the medium or presentation format. Instructional designers can reuse content developed by others and present this in multiple media formats. This perspective is presented by Chapman and Hall (2001), where it is suggested that a learning management content system is needed to identify, collect, organize, and present content to learners. Such a repository would create, store, reuse, and manage learning content, including more traditionally viewed libraries and information resources.

Anido and colleagues (2002) discussed the developments in learning technology standardization with the purpose being the reuse and interoperation among learning systems. Educational metadata provide a means to facilitate the location of learning resources, with the users then being able to find resources applicable to their own contexts. The Shared Content Object Reference Model (SCORM) provides a set of interrelated specifications supporting the interoperability, accessibility, and reusability of Web-based learning content. The effort, the results of which are distributed through the Advanced Distributed Learning (ADL) Initiative, is focused on meeting the U.S. Department of Defense's requirements for Web-based learning content (ADL, 2002).

5. References:

Advanced Distributed Learning (ADL). (2002). *SCORM overview.* Retrieved December 13, 2002, from http://www.adlnet.org

Anido, L. E., Fernandez, M. J., Caeiro, M., Santos, J. M., Rodriguez, J. S., & Llamas, M. (2002). Educational metadata and brokerage for learning resources. *Computers and Education, 38,* 351–374.

Chapman, B., & Hall, B. (2001) *Learning content management systems.* Sunnyvale, CA: bran-

don-hall.com. Retrieved July 18, 2002, from
www.brandon-hall.com/learnconmansy.html

6. Glossary: **Interoperation/Interoperability:** The ability of
hardware or software components to work
together effectively. [American Society for
Training and Development. (n.d.). Glossary
(compiled by E. Kaplan-Leiserson). *Learning
circuits.* Alexandria, VA: Author. Retrieved July
20, 2002, from http://www.learningcircuits
.org/glossary.html]

Learning Content Management System (LCMS):
A software application that allows trainers
and training directors to manage both the
administrative and content-related functions of training. An LCMS combines the
course management capabilities of an LMS
(learning management system) with the
content creation and storage capabilities of
a CMS (content management system).
Includes learning objects, the reusable,
media-independent chunks of information
used as modular building blocks for e-learning content. [American Society for Training
and Development. (n.d.). Glossary (compiled by E. Kaplan-Leiserson). *Learning circuits.* Alexandria, VA: Author. Retrieved July
20, 2002, from http://www.learningcircuits
.org/glossary.html]

Metadata: Information about content that allows
it to be stored and retrieved from a database; learning objects are most effective
when organized by a metadata classification
system and stored in a data repository such
as an LCMS. [American Society for Training
and Development. (n.d.). Glossary (compiled by E. Kaplan-Leiserson). *Learning circuits.* Alexandria, VA: Author. Retrieved July
20, 2002, from http://www.learningcircuits
.org/glossary.html]

7. User: Program manager

STRATEGIES BASED ON STUDENT SUPPORT SERVICES

1. Guideline: Provide an appropriate learner support environment with assistance in counseling, scheduling and registration, problem solving, mentoring, delivery of course materials, and maintenance of appropriate records and transcripts.

2. Guideline based on: Expert opinion

3. Degree of confidence: Medium

4. Comments: Student support services are central to the success of a distance learning program. These services include providing advisement, counseling, materials and textbook delivery, test materials delivery, and examination proctoring with service policies that should be of the same standard as those in nondistance modes (Gellman-Danley & Fetzner, 1998). From the perspective of post-distance learning course completion, support services relate to the maintenance of records and delivery of verification for courses and training, such as the forwarding of course transcripts.

The eArmyU, officially named the Army University Access Online (AUAO), provides for counseling, online course selection, virtual mentoring, delivery of a "tech pack" of hardware and software, tutorials, and career guidance (Lorenzo, 2002). Wagner (2001) further expanded this discussion and presented a description of the types of services to be provided in a virtual student support system, including an explanation of requirements, accurate record keeping, FAQs, study skills information, policies, how to get computer access and technical support, and an online bookstore. One-to-one advisement can be supported through e-mail, chat rooms, and listserv approaches.

5. References: Gellman-Danley, B., & Fetzner, M. J. (1998). Asking the really tough questions: Policy issues for distance education. *Online Journal of Distance Learning Administration, 1*(1). Retrieved

July 20, 2002, from http://www.westga.edu/
~distance/danley11/html

Lorenzo, G. (2002, May/June). eArmyU and the
future of distance education. *The Technology
Source* [Online]. Lansing: Michigan Virtual
University. Retrieved July 21, 2002, from
http://ts.mivu.org/deafult.asp?show
=article&id=998

Wagner, L. (2001). Virtual advising: Delivering
student services. *Online Journal of Distance
Learning Administration, 4*(3). Retrieved July
21, 2002, from http://www.westga.edu/~dis-
tance/ojdla/fall43/wagner43.html

6. Glossary:

FAQs: Frequently asked questions; a file established for public discussion groups containing questions and answers new users often
ask. [American Society for Training and
Development. (n.d.). Glossary (compiled by
E. Kaplan-Leiserson). *Learning circuits.* Alexandria, VA: Author. Retrieved July 20, 2002,
from http://www.learningcircuits.org/glos-
sary.html]

7. User:

Program manager

STRATEGIES BASED ON INSTRUCTOR COMPETENCY

1. Guideline:

Instructors must have the necessary skills and
competencies appropriate for teaching via distance learning.

2. Guideline based on:

Expert opinion

3. Degree of confidence:

Medium

4. Comments:

Instructors need assistance in the transition from
traditional to online teaching. Rockwell,
Schauer, Fritz, and Marz (2000) provided the
results from a survey of the need for training,
assistance, and support to develop distance learning. Respondents noted the need for assistance
in developing instructional experiences that supported interactive learning experiences, develop-

ing and improving instructional materials, and applying selected technologies. Bonk (2002) also conducted survey research related to the use of e-learning in the corporate world and other training settings. He identified a number of approaches used for supporting the instructor. These included e-mail support, online help and tutorials, internal support from other staff, attendance at conferences or workshops, and use of local experts for supporting design and development efforts. He emphasized the need for organizational support in terms of training for designers, and the need for their certification.

Clay (1999) provided an overview of the components of an effective development and support program for distance education instructors. Types of effective training are noted, such as group sessions, one-on-one lab sessions, mentorships, observation, and scheduled discussion sessions among peers. Typical distance learning training topics are listed, with some additional topics that are sometimes overlooked—that is, the need for backup and contingency plans, and the need to address copyright issues.

5. References:

Bonk, C. J. (2002). *Online training in an online world.* Bloomington, IN: CourseShare.com. Retrieved July 26, 2002, from http://www.jonesknowledge.com/corporate/index.php

Clay, M. (1999). Development of training and support programs for distance education instructors. *Online Journal of Distance Learning Administration, 2*(3). Retrieved July 26, 2002, from http://www.westga.edu~distance/clay23.html

Crumpacker, N. (2001). Faculty pedagogical approach, skill, and motivation in today's distance education milieu. *Online Journal of Distance Learning Administration, 4*(4). Retrieved July 26, 2002, from http://www.westga.edu/~distance/ojdla/winter44/crumpacker44.html

Rockwell, K., Schauer, J., Fritz, S. M., & Marz, D. B. (2000). Faculty education, assistance and support needed to deliver education via distance. *Online Journal of Distance Learning Administration, 3*(2). Retrieved July 26, 2002, from http://www.westga.edu/~distance/rockwell32.html

6. Glossary:	None
7. User:	Program manager

STRATEGIES BASED ON LEARNER CHARACTERISTICS

1. Guideline:	Design distance learning taking into consideration learner characteristics.
2. Guideline based on:	Research
3. Degree of confidence:	High
4. Comments:	Distance learning is a form of self-directed or self-regulated learning, and as such, students need to manage, control, and evaluate their learning behavior. Learners require motivation, appropriate learning strategies, and time management skills. The opinions of learners in regard to distance learning can be an important factor in success (Valenta, Therriault, Dieter, & Mrtek, 2001).

Along the same line of research, Christensen, Anakwe, and Kessler (2001) posited the effect of technology perception on students' receptivity toward distance learning. Providing distance learning per se is not perceived as viable unless it is coupled with its perceived usefulness to learning. It should be noted that receptivity toward distance learning is enhanced by interactivity that provides increased support, guidance, feedback, and small-group learning. Lim (2001) indicated that computer self-efficacy was a predictive variable, and a positive relation existed between satisfaction and future distance learning enrollment intent.

5. References:

Bandura, A. (1994). Self-efficacy. In V. S. Ramachaudran (Ed.), *Encyclopedia of human behavior* (Vol. 4, pp. 71–81). New York: Academic Press. Retrieved January 20, 2004, from http://www.emory.edu/EDUCATION/mfp/BanEncy.html

Christensen, E. W., Anakwe, U. P., & Kessler, E. H. (2001). Receptivity to distance learning: The effect of technology, reputation, constraints, and learning preferences. *Journal of Research on Computing in Education, 33,* 263–279.

Lim, C. K. (2001). Computer self-efficacy, academic self-concept, and other predictors of satisfaction and future participation of adult distance learners. *American Journal of Distance Education, 13*(2), 41–51.

Valenta, A., Therriault, D., Dieter, M., & Mrtek, R. (2001). Identifying student attitudes and learning styles in distance education. *Journal of Asynchronous Learning Networks, 5*(2). Retrieved July 26, 2002, from http://www.aln.org/alnweb/journal/Vol5_issue2/Valenta/Valenta.html

6. Glossary:

Self-efficacy: Defined as people's beliefs about their capabilities to produce designated levels of performance that exercise influence over events that affect their lives. Self-efficacy beliefs determine how people feel, think, motivate themselves, and behave. A strong sense of efficacy enhances human accomplishment and personal well-being (Bandura, 1994).

7. User:

Instructional designer

STRATEGIES BASED ON INSTRUCTIONAL DESIGN

1. Guideline:

Incorporate effective learning features into distance learning instructional design, examples of which include interactivity, timely feedback, and use of small learning groups.

2. Guideline based on: Research

3. Degree of confidence: High

4. Comment: A criticism of distance learning has been on the variability of the overall quality of online courses. This variation in quality is due to the lack of adequate, timely, and consistent feedback, the lack of interactivity, and the lack of a virtual community. Thus, much of the literature reflects the need to employ timely feedback, to use active learning to promote learner engagement, and to develop virtual learning communities.

Picciano (2002) noted that the literature is extensive on the topic of interactivity and concluded that instructor responsiveness and feedback, instructor-to-learner interaction, and learner-to-learner interaction are keys to success. Robyler and Ekhaml (2000) developed a rubric for determining the level of interactivity in a distance learning course.

Haythornthwaite, Kazmer, Robins, and Shoemaker (2000) conducted a detailed analysis of a distance program in terms of the development of a virtual community and how learners define and maintain this community. The researchers provided recommendations to support virtual communities, namely developing initial bonding through an intensive proximity-based "live" class session, monitoring and supporting interaction and participation such as through examining chat room sessions, and providing multiple technology-based communication means for interaction.

5. References: Haythornthwaite, C., Kazmer, M. M., Robins, J., & Shoemaker, S. (2000). Community development among distance learners: Temporal and technological dimensions. *Journal of Computer Media Communications, 6*(1). Retrieved August 11, 2002, from http://www.ascusc.org/jcmc/vol6/issue1/haythornthwaite.html

Picciano, A. G. (2002). Beyond student perceptions: Issues of interaction, presence, and performance in an online course. *Journal of Asynchronous Learning Networks, 6*(1). Retrieved August 8, 2002, from http://www.aln.org/alnweb/journal/Vol6_issue1/6_1picciano.htm

Rafaeli, S., & Sudweeks, F. (1997). Networked interactivity. *Journal of Computer Media Communications, 2*(4). Retrieved August 11, 2002, from http://www.ascusc.org/jcmc/vol2/issue4/rafaeli_sudweeks.html

Robyler, M. D., & Ekhaml, L. (2000). How interactive are your distance courses? A rubric for assessing interactivity in distance courses. *Online Journal of Distance Learning Administration, 3*(2). Retrieved November 11, 2002, from http://www.westga.edu/~distance/robyler32.html

6. Glossary:

Active learning: Any approach that engages learners by matching instruction to the learner's interests, understanding and development level. Often includes hands-on and authentic activities. [*Glossary of instructional strategies.* (n.d.). Beaverton, OR: Plasma-Link Web Services. Retrieved December 13, 2002, from http://glossary.plasmalink.com/glossary.html]

Interaction: Refers to communication, participation, and feedback between learners with other learners and/or instructors/tutors. [Yacci, M. (n.d.). *Interactivity demystified: A structural definition for distance education and intelligent CBT.* Retrieved November 11, 2002, from http://www.it.rit.edu/~may/inte.pdf]

Virtual community: Also known as an online community; a meeting place for people on the Internet. Designed to facilitate interaction and collaboration among people who share common interests and needs. Online communities can be open to all or by membership only and may or may not offer moderator tools. [American Society for Training and Development. (n.d.). Glossary (compiled by E. Kaplan-Leiserson). *Learning circuits.* Alexandria, VA: Author. Retrieved July 20, 2002, from http://www.learningcircuits.org/glossary.html]

7. *User:*   Instructional designer

CHAPTER 9

TRANSITION AND IMPLEMENTATION ISSUES

Harold F. O'Neil
University of Southern California/CRESST

The suggested steps in the implementation process for the guidelines are shown in Table 9.1. The process begins with a series of briefs to the "customer" and is completed with a formative evaluation.

Table 9.1.   Guidelines Implementation Process

Visit customer headquarters to brief results and select test sites.

Specify how to scale up (e.g., copyright permission for reproduction, knowledge management lessons learned—see, e.g., Davenport & Glaser, 2002; Hansen, Nohria, & Tierney, 1999).

Scale up procedures for use (e.g., "books" are paper-based at site and searchable database with two-page guidelines is at a portal).

Set up guidelines update procedures (e.g., every 2 years).

Set up reach-back procedures (e.g., availability of experts).

Set up and conduct formative evaluation.

What Works in Distance Learning: Guidlines, pages 143–144
Copyright © 2005 by Information Age Publishing
All rights of reproduction in any form reserved.

Our planned approach to formative evaluation of the guidelines is shown in Table 9.2. The procedure involves multiple steps, some of them iterative. We begin the formative evaluation process by checking whether the design of portal use is congruent with specifications, and we end with implementing revisions.

Table 9.2.   Formative Evaluation Activity

1. Check the system design, including portal use, against its specifications.
2. Check the validity of instructional strategies embedded in the system (e.g., navigational strategies) against research literature.
3. Conduct feasibility review with the users.
   • Are right tasks being trained?
4. Conduct feasibility tests with the users.
   • One-on-one testing
   • Small-group testing
5. Do experts and novices differ in performance?
6. Does more training lead to better performance?
7. Implement revisions.

Initially the focus was on guidelines to facilitate individual learning (e.g., self-regulation and motivation). Our next steps for our research program in this area are shown in Table 9.3. We are now developing guidelines on Team Training and Team Performance Measurement. Next, cases or lessons for each new set of guidelines will be designed and developed. Then, an informative system will be created and evaluated.

Table 9.3.   Next Steps

Team Training Guidelines

Team Performance Measurement Guidelines

Create lessons for each new set of guidelines

Develop information system for guidelines and lessons

Conduct formative evaluation of information system

REFERENCES

Davenport, T. H., & Glaser, J. (2002). Just-in-time delivery comes to knowledge management. *Harvard Business Review, 80*(7), 107–111.

Hansen, M. T., Nohria, N., & Tierney, T. (1999). What's your strategy for managing knowledge? *Harvard Business Review, 77*(2), 106–116.

Printed in the United States
48273LVS00001B/257

9 781593 112608